A Writer's Guide

— TO —

ACTIVE
SETTING

MARY BUCKHAM

WRITER'S DIGEST BOOKS

An imprint of Penguin Random House LLC
penguinrandomhouse.com

ISBN 978-1-59963-930-7

Edited by Cris Freese
Designed by Alexis Brown

146056540

DEDICATION

For the writers who want to expand their understanding of the craft of writing!

ACKNOWLEDGMENTS

Writing any book does not happen in a vacuum, especially a how-to craft book. I'd like to thank the hundreds and hundreds of writing students who helped define the assignments and the need to explore how to better use Setting in our novels. I'd also like to thank my early readers, all writers who gave invaluable feedback on the format and content of this book: Laurie G. Adams, Kat Jorgensen, Elizabeth Gibson, Theresa Rogers, Ellen Russell, Debbie Kaufman, Deborah K. Andersen, and Laurel Wilczek. A special thank you to Dr. Patrick Maher, former Chair of the Australian Writers Guild, for his invaluable insights. Any of the great advice I did not take was my fault alone. A special thanks to Dianna Love, writer extraordinaire and a good friend who has always been there for one last eagle-eyed look. And to my husband, Jim Buckham, who makes all things possible in my world. And last, but not least, thanks to my readers. Without you, I'd have no craft to teach. Thank you!

TABLE OF CONTENTS

PART ONE

CHARACTERIZATION & SENSORY DETAIL

PART TWO

EMOTION, CONFLICT, & BACKSTORY

PART THREE

ANCHORING, ACTION, SETTING AS A CHARACTER, & MORE

Foreword

Crafting a good book takes a lot of hard work.

Crafting a *great* book demands even more.

I want every novel I write to be better than my last one. That's intimidating, but very possible as long as I continue to push myself to grow as a writer. I believe writers are born with talent, but exceptional writing comes from studying craft ... and studying some more. Writers with discipline and dedication will quite often outpace those who depend solely on talent every time they sit down to write.

Our job as writers is to give the reader an emotionally satisfying experience, but that experience is in jeopardy if the reader begins to skim.

Why does a reader skim?

Because the words become boring. There are two opportunities to bore a reader even in the most active story—introspection and setting. Those two often go hand in hand, which is good and bad news. The bad news is that you have twice as much opportunity to lose your reader, but the good news is you can use setting to ramp up the tension and emotion to pull your reader even deeper into your story.

For too long, setting has been ignored.

Wait ... that's not actually true. Unfortunately, the setting is often described at great length. Some writers spend paragraph after paragraph detailing the world the protagonist has entered, as if the character paused to do a mental rundown of everything around.

Great writing instead weaves setting throughout story just as emotional arc is woven through every scene. I've said for many years that Mary Buckham creates brilliant settings in her books. Some might say it's because she's traveled all over the world, but rather than droning on with flowery descriptions like those found in travel brochures, she has the skill to plunk a reader right in the middle of a location.

When setting is introduced this way, the reader feels the setting as it develops. Crafting stories in a way that drops the reader in the middle of a scene with precision and emotion is both a gift and a skill, one that can be learned.

Mary has shared this gift through workshops she teaches in the US and internationally. I've referred many writers to her workshops and all have raved about Mary's ability to provide instruction in such a way that writers see immediate improvement in their stories. Still, if she taught for the next hundred years, she would never be able to reach every writer, which is why putting all that valuable information into a book is the best of news for all of us.

Writers everywhere can now benefit from Mary Buckham's clever instruction. *A Writer's Guide to Active Setting* is for the writer who wants to break out of the pack and make a name in publishing by engaging readers so powerfully that they always come back for more.

Anyone can create a setting in great detail, painting a beautiful scene using description, but a master pulls a reader deep into that scene by drawing on emotional context.

How does that happen?

The easiest way for me to answer that question is by suggesting you read this book.

—Dianna Love, *New York Times* best-selling author

Introduction

Setting can be one of the most underused tools in a writer's toolbox, but it shouldn't be.

Setting involves much more than stringing together a list of adjectives or dumping a chunk of visual clues to orient the reader. It can create the world of your story, show characterization, add conflict, slow or speed up your pacing, add or decrease tension, relate a character's backstory, thread in emotion, and more. Some authors are known for creating Settings that are so deeply integrated into the story that when readers step away, they still find themselves in the place described on the page.

Think of Setting as the stage that contains your story—it should be as important as any character, whether you choose to write sparsely or in great detail. The Setting orients readers to the geography, climate, social context, time of the story's events, foreshadowing of unfolding events, architecture, and much more. When handled well, Setting can also have an impact on your readers' thoughts and your characters' actions, thus moving the story forward.

If handled poorly, Setting description can thwart or frustrate to the point where the reader wants to set the book down and walk away.

Setting can add so much to your story world, or it can add nothing. In creating Active Setting, you can develop subtext in your writing—a deeper way for your reader to experience your story.

Instead of simply describing a place or thing for the sake of description, we'll look closely at how to maximize what you are showing the reader. You'll learn how to verbally illustrate a place and where to insert this information so the reader will understand the intention of your scenes and be pulled deeper into the story. In chapter one, we'll look at using Setting to reveal your characters and to add sensory details.

You'll also learn how to make sure your reader focuses only on details that are pertinent to the story.

NOTE: The details of your Setting must matter to your story.

For example, if you're showing the reader a room in a house, that room, and the details in that room, should show characterization, conflict, emotion, or foreshadowing. The description should be there for a reason instead of simply describing placement of objects in space.

Let's start with an overview of what Setting is and what it can be.

Overview

In this book we'll focus on keeping in mind three key elements in crafting Setting to make it active:

1. You need to create the world of your story.
2. Each character in your story experiences the story world differently.
3. Your story world involves more than one sense.

What this means is that your role as a writer is to create the world of your story so that the reader not only sees it, but experiences every important detail.

Active Setting means using your Setting descriptions to add more to your story than a passive visual reference. This book will explain in greater detail how to make this happen regardless of what type of story you're crafting.

NOTE: If the details don't add to the story, leave them out. Every word choice you make in your story should be intentional and focus the reader on what you want. Don't waste their focus on trivial details.

Regardless of whether you're writing about a famous place that millions have seen in pictures or experienced in person, your character's perceptions of that world are what matters in your story. You're not writing about any living room, small town, or large city; you are writing about a specific living room, small town, or large city and why those Settings matter to your character.

Pull the reader into your story by allowing them to experience the Setting on a deeper level. This can be the difference between standing on a beach facing the Pacific Ocean, feeling the sand beneath your bare toes, inhaling the scent of tangy salt spray, and hearing the roar and slam of the waves against the shore versus looking at a postcard.

Learning to write Active Setting is as easy as knowing when and where you want to ramp up your Setting details and why.

I've had the privilege to work with thousands of writers in all genres over the years and to see them take the blah or non-existent Setting of their stories and make their passive Setting description work harder and do so much more than simply describe a place. That's my wish for every writer who takes the time to study Active Setting.

PART ONE

CHARACTERIZATION

SENSORY DETAIL

01

Getting Started with Active Setting

Throughout this book we'll be looking at how you can ramp up elements of your story by how you use or do not use your Setting. We'll start with an overview of why Setting matters to a story and see examples from published authors showing, in a variety of genres, how they maximized Setting in their novels. Always keep in mind that Setting is more than describing a place.

NOTE: Active Setting means using your Setting details to work harder and smarter.

First, you should focus on what seems like a basic assumption.

Your reader has never been in your world—wherever your world is.

It doesn't matter if it's New York City and most of your readers live in Manhattan; your reader has never been in *your* world. The Setting and world you'll paint on the page are more than a travelogue or a list of street names.

Not everything that a character sees, smells, tastes, or touches needs to end up in your final manuscript, but it's a place to start. For example, a point of view (POV) character (the person whose thoughts, emotions, background, and worldview through which the reader experiences the story) who is miserable in a school environment will not see or notice the same items as a POV character who finds school a sanctuary and the center of her world.

As the author, you need to focus the reader on what's key about your POV character's world Setting and then bring that information to life through word choices, details, and how you thread those details together.

NOTE: The details you choose to share must matter. (Yes, I'm hammering home this point.)

Your reader should not be focused on something that is not pertinent to your story. Why? You're wasting an opportunity to make your Setting show more than a place or an item simply because you as the author find it interesting. Make the Setting reveal more than that. Too much narrative, which is what Setting is in large chunks, slows your pacing.

You are not just working with objects in space—you're creating a world. When you make characters interact with the space they're in, you can make those few words become more than just descriptors. Doing so turns these words into ways the reader can grasp the world as the character experiences it.

POOR EXAMPLE: Sue walked into her mother's living room, past the couch and the coffee table, to sit down in a chair.

What is the above sentence showing you? Revealing to you? Letting you experience? Not much, it's simply moving a character through space.

REWRITTEN EXAMPLE: Sue walked into the gilt-and-silk living room of her mother's home, gagging on the clash of floral odors: lilac potpourri, jasmine candles, lavender sachets. Did her mom even smell the cloying thickness anymore? Did she ever try to glance beyond the draped and beribboned window coverings that kept the room in perpetual dusk? Or was she using the white-on-white colors and velvet textures to hide from the real world? With a sigh, Sue sank into a designer chair and hoped she could crawl out of it sooner rather than later.

OR:

> **REWRITTEN EXAMPLE:** Sue walked into the heart of her child-hood home, remembering playing cowboys and Indians behind the worn tweed couch, building tents by draping sheets over the nicked coffee table, hiding behind the cotton drapes that were now replaced by newer blinds. Her grandmother used to shudder when she deigned to visit the house, but Sue's mom didn't care. Now she'd no longer be knitting in her easy chair or patting the sagging couch for a tell-me-all-about-it session.

See? The painted details allow you to experience a lot more than simply seeing a room. That's the power of Active Setting.

Let's look at another example: Four brief sentences that quickly pull the reader into a bar scene, only this bar is in an urban fantasy novel and the bar is populated with vampires. But the author, Marjorie M. Liu, wants to make it clear that the world between humans and preter-naturals is not clearly delineated. This bar could be any bar, anywhere, and the reader should be aware of that fact. Examine specifically how the details, especially the sensory details, make this Setting, and thus the scene, come alive.

> … and stepped sideways to the battered bar, its surface scarred and mauled by years of hard elbows and broken glass. Ashtrays over-flowed. Bottles clustered. Everything, sticky with fingerprints: even the air, marked, cut with smoke and sweat.
> —Marjorie M. Liu, *The Iron Hunt*

Now let's pull apart all the sensory details and see why they ramp up what many writers would have ignored.

> … and stepped sideways to the battered bar, [*This is a visual that's very specific and tells the reader where the character is, but the author doesn't stop here.*] its surface scarred and mauled [*Powerful action verbs.*] by years of hard elbows and broken glass. [*Here she brings*

home the point—battered bar *is the initial image. Then the reader is focused on its surface,* scarred and mauled. *Finally the reason the bar got to this point*—via hard elbows and broken glass. *The author layers the details to bring home her point.*] Ashtrays overflowed. [*Visual and smell detail.*] Bottles clustered. [*The author didn't stop with a row of bottles, but the action verb gives an image of bottles clustered together as if for mutual support.*] Everything, sticky with fingerprints: [*Tactile detail.*] even the air, marked, cut with smoke and sweat. [*And more smells.*]

In just a few sentences the reader is with the POV character, standing in this bar, experiencing, smelling, hearing, and feeling that situation.

Anchoring the Reader

So how do you initially show the Setting in the scene? One thing to remember is that the reader does need a quick "anchoring," probably in the first few paragraphs of a new scene or new chapter, or a change in location. Where are we? What time of day is it? Is it quiet or noisy? What is the quality of light?

> **NOTE:** The use of light can show time change. Instead of telling the reader it's twenty minutes later, show them by the cast of late-afternoon shadows, the glare of the sun directly overhead, the quieting of the birds as dusk falls.

The reader will be mentally asking these questions, and the longer you keep the information from them, the less they will focus on what you want them to focus on. The reader will become more removed from the story and the characters, and instead be trying to figure out the where, when, who, or why.

Once you've established or anchored the reader into the *where* of your story, using a strong Setting description, you do not need to continue to embellish and rehash a Setting. Let the characters interact with

A Writer's Guide to Active Setting

the Setting, move through it, pick things up and brush past them, once the reader knows the character is in a place already described.

Whenever there's a Setting introduction that's different for the POV character, or for the reader, you should use a few words of description to orient or anchor the reader into the new environment. For example, it's human nature to notice what's changed—you might not notice an object on your mantel every day, but you do notice when it's missing. If an object, like a beloved photograph, was foreshadowed earlier in the story, you can now show that it's missing, which allows the reader to mentally see the rest of the room that you've already established and know where the POV character is. We're in that character's skin, seeing what was once there and now is not. So instead of starting this scene with the character re-entering the living room, you show the reader that the first thing the character notices when she enters the living room is the gap on the mantel: The space where her mother's photo was. *Bam!* We're in that living room without spending a lot of time redescribing what the reader has already been shown.

Look at how Laura Anne Gilman orients the reader as to where the character is physically in space and gives a hint of the protagonist's backstory, characterization of two different characters, and a hint of potential conflict between characters through her description of a room. All in only one paragraph!

> The only way to describe J's place was "warm." Rosewood furniture against cream-colored walls, and touches of dark blue and flannel gray everywhere, broken by the occasional bit of foam green from his Chinese pottery collection. You'd have thought I'd have grown up to be Uber Society Girl, not pixie-Goth, in these surroundings. Even my bedroom—now turned back into its original use as a library—had the same feel of calm wealth to it, no matter how many pop-culture posters I put up or how dark I painted the walls.
> —Laura Anne Gilman, *Hard Magic*

Now let's dissect that paragraph to see the power of the individual parts.

The only way to describe J's place was "warm." [*Subjective emotion from the POV character that gives a hint of her relationship with the home's owner. Plus we are able to get a quick sense of the feel of a place; we know when we've been in a warm or cool room even if we don't have too many details yet.*] Rosewood furniture against cream-colored walls, and touches of dark blue and flannel gray everywhere, [*Notice the pieces of furniture are not described because it's not important to know there's a couch or two chairs in the room. It's more important to get a sense of the owner of the room by his choice of subtle and understated colors and the wood—rosewood is a world away from oak or distressed pine. We're getting a glimpse into the world of the secondary character here.*] broken by the occasional bit of foam green from his Chinese pottery collection. [*Here, because collecting Chinese pottery is not the same as collecting baseball cards or stamps, the reader has another image of the wealth and refinement of the home's owner.*] You'd have thought I'd have grown up to be Uber Society Girl, not pixie-Goth, in these surroundings. [*Now the reader is focused on the differences between the POV character's sense of self and the home's owner by use of contrast. This is (or was) her home, yet it's clear she does not see herself as belonging.*] Even my bedroom—now turned back into its original use as a library—had the same feel of calm wealth to it, no matter how many pop-culture posters I put up or how dark I painted the walls. [*This hints at conflict and foreshadowing.*]

Through her specific word choices and the objects she's chosen to comment on, Gilman has deepened her world building between these two characters in the series. We are now seeing where the POV character came from and where her mentor still lives through the use of Setting description. The author's word choices, pointing out the contrast between *calm wealth, pop-culture posters*, and dark-painted walls, reveals to the reader the POV sense of not belonging in the world in which she was raised, which is a key theme in this story.

Let's look at another example approaching Setting from a rough draft version to the final version.

FIRST DRAFT: The wardens led me to a room and left me there.

Pretty bland description. The reader is not deep into this character's POV because the character is not experiencing the room.

> **NOTE:** Showing the room through deeper POV allows the reader to experience the room on a more immediate level. The reader is in the room with the character.

> **SECOND DRAFT:** I'm conducted to a room and left alone. It's the richest place I've ever been in.

Better because now we're given a little more insight into what the POV character is feeling based on the response to the room. But we still have no idea why the character feels this way. Nor can we see the room. Plus instead of being shown the place, we're only told about it.

Let's see how Suzanne Collins used the Setting to enhance the opening of her story:

> Once inside, I'm conducted to a room and left alone. It's the richest place I've ever been in, with thick deep carpets and a velvet couch and chairs. I know velvet because my mother has a dress with a collar made of the stuff. When I sit on the couch, I can't help running my fingers over the fabric repeatedly. It helps to calm me as I try to prepare for the next hour. The time allotted for the tributes to say goodbye to their loved ones.
> —Suzanne Collins, *The Hunger Games*

Here we have more Setting details that allow the author to show some characterization of the POV character and reveal emotions based on her interaction with this room, all by adding just a few more details of Setting. The Setting information is also bracketed by the emotion of the paragraph, like this:

- The first sentence is all about choreography. She's moving the POV character through space from one location to another.

- The second sentence starts with internalization that cues the reader into how the POV character feels and ends on Setting.
- The third sentence picks up the hint of Setting detail from the previous sentence with a key word—*velvet*—and reveals a hint of backstory.
- The fourth sentence expands on the Setting imagery and adds body language to show emotion.
- The fifth sentence brings the reader back around to the larger story question of what's going to happen next to this character.

Can you see how the author uses Setting to give the reader a breathing space, deepen the emotional stakes of the story, and then move the story forward?

Here's another example. This passage is from a debut author who, instead of telling, shows the reader that the POV character has arrived at her husband's new home. It's a home that doesn't look like much but is better than anything she's ever had.

> We drove up to the last cottage on the back end of a strip of land. It had funny brown shingles peeling away from the clapboard, and the roof looked a little saggy. I had only lived in a trailer all my life, and this was a real house.

—Joyce Keller Walsh, *Strummin' the Banjo Moon*

In the above example, the author did an outstanding job of letting the reader see a house that's not all that great—*back end, strip of land, peeling shingles, saggy roof*—since these negative words are qualified—*funny brown, a little saggy*—then follows with the clear qualification that the character had never lived in a real house before. This allows the reader to see that, for this particular character, this not so great house was better than she'd ever had. A whole lot of characterization is revealed via Setting.

A Writer's Guide to Active Setting

NOTE: As in painting, when you use a cool ultramarine color, and then dab a spot of warm orange on the blue, it makes it pop. The reader can suddenly be "popped" deeper into the POV character's head with a clearer picture of how she sees and experiences the world.

Subtext in Setting

Have you ever attended an event with a friend or family member and later, in discussing the event, discovered that based on the friend's description, you each seemed to have been at a totally different event? Mystery-writer Agatha Christie used this ability to great effect. She allowed her characters to focus in on what matters to them in one of her Hercule Poirot stories, *Cards on the Table*. The Belgian detective ask half-a-dozen participants of a party to describe the room where the murder took place. All of the characters, because they come from different backgrounds with different interests, they describe highlights of the room from totally different perspectives. One notes the very valuable and esoteric collectibles scattered around on the tabletops. Another, a soldier who spent many years in the Middle East, could tell the detective the tribal names of the woven rugs on the floor; another character saw the room in terms of colors, and another could describe the type of period furniture.

Now if the reader had not already "seen" the entire room—in all its detail—through the detective's eyes, but saw only the small snippets from the individual secondary characters, the reader might see only a room with knick-knacks or just a room with carpets, but no furniture. By letting the audience see the whole room through Poirot's POV first, and then revisiting the room through each character's POV, the reader is led to solve the mystery of who killed the victim because only one character "saw" the weapon that was at hand.

NOTE: The Setting you create will be seen only through one character at a time, so it's important to make sure that what your character sees matters.

Let's revisit an earlier point to see how a POV character that is miserable in a school environment will not see or notice the same items as a POV character who finds that same school a sanctuary and the center of his world. The first example will be through the POV of a character visiting the principal's office. See how quickly you get the emotional tenor of the passage and what else the passage reveals about this character?

> **EXAMPLE ONE:** I strolled down the empty hallway, hearing the slap of my hard soles against the worn linoleum, remembering the all-too-many times I had crawled this same route to Mrs. Pendragon's office.
>
> One slap; you're in trouble.
>
> Two slaps; shouldn't have got caught.
>
> Third slap; loser.
>
> The stink of sweat and cheap cleaning supplies gagged me back then and did the same today. The flicker of a fluorescent light sent a shiver down my back. But I wasn't sixteen anymore and heading down the fast slope of trouble even as I stopped before the closed wood-and-glass door of the principal's office.

Did you notice the key details used? Word choices—*empty, slap, hard soles, worn*—and sensory details (sounds, smells, visual cues) and then ending on a story question raised via the POV character's internalization about the Setting. The above example is all it took to layer a lot of subtext on the page using Setting.

Here's the second example.

> **EXAMPLE TWO:** The sounds caught me first. Laughter ricocheting off the metal lockers, the low rumble of a guy's voice changing timbre, the kick slam of tennis shoes hitting stubborn locker doors. Then came the memories. Hand-lettered signs promising the next

school dance, an orange and black banner urging the football or basketball team on to new heights, the crepe paper streamers still hanging from the last Pep Con. I'd been gone twenty years and in the space of twenty footsteps this hall tugged me back to the best times of my life.

A world of difference based solely by what the POV character is seeing in this Setting and his response to it. That's the power of Active Setting.

> **NOTE:** Subtext is the underlying message the reader receives from a passage. Dialogue or action may say one thing: all appears to be fine, but the reader understands from other cues—such as the Setting—that the subtext is saying something else.

Setting the Stage

Remember to think of Setting as the stage that contains your story. Keeping the Setting lean and mean is important, but it can be dangerous to stuff all the details into one paragraph that's describing only Setting. Often this will bring your pacing to a halt. However, this method can work if your pacing is so strong that all the reader wants to do is get back into the story. For example:

> It was a sunny April day. But Stark Street looked dreary. Pages from a newspaper cart wheeled down the street and banked against curbs and the cement stoops of cheerless row houses. Gang slogans were spray painted on brick fronts. An occasional building had been burned and gutted, the windows blackened and boarded. Small businesses squatted between the row houses. Andy's Bar & Grill, Stark Street Garage, Stan's Appliances, Omar's Meat Market.
> —Janet Evanovich, *Seven Up*

Let's break down the Setting in the above example into specific elements. First, Evanovich describes this Setting in depth because it is the first time her POV character arrives at this new location and she wants to make her character's world vivid to the reader. This is one of the places (pun intended) where the reader will allow the author to slow the pacing a bit in order to see where the character is. Doing so allows the reader to feel and be in that place with the character.

Now let's examine how Evanovich uses her descriptive phrases to create the world of New Jersey bounty-hunter Stephanie Plum. The author does not leave it to the reader to guess about the neighborhood; she uses key details to make it come alive.

> It was a sunny April day. [*Orient the reader to time of year and a general sense of time of day. It's not night or early morning, given that it's sunny. Also, this acts as a contrast to what comes next, which makes the reader take notice.*] But Stark Street looked dreary. [*The author "tells" (versus shows) what the POV character thinks about the Setting, but then goes on to show with specific details. Telling alone is shorthand, and too much of it holds the reader at a distance from the story. But when telling is used with showing, it can be effective. By telling us, Evanovich gives us a direction from which we can interpret what we're going to see next on this street.*] Pages from a newspaper cartwheeled [*Action verbs, as opposed to passive "to be" verbs, make stronger, more concrete images in the reader's mind.*] down the street and banked [*Action verb.*] against curbs and the cement stoops of cheerless row houses. [*Specific types of houses—these are not bungalows or 1980s ranch style homes. The reader can start to see the Setting more clearly by this small detail.*] Gang slogans were spray-painted on brick fronts. [*Very specific details showing the neglect of the area and how the buildings were made, which offers a distinct image. Change this one detail, from brick to concrete or faded lap siding, and you have a very different image of the houses.*] An occasional building had been burned and gutted, the windows blackened and boarded. [*By repeating the terms—burned and gutted, blackened and boarded—the author hammers home the images in this specific world.*] Small businesses squatted [*Action verb.*] between the row

houses. Andy's Bar & Grill, Stark Street Garage, Stan's Appliances, Omar's Meat Market. [*Notice the male names most common in the 1950s. This tells the reader these are small, family-owned, and probably older businesses.*]

Now what if Evanovich had simply written:

> **INITIAL DRAFT:** It was a sunny April day. But Stark Street looked dreary. We looked for Omar's Meat Market and found it.

The reader would have felt rushed, and, while knowing they were on a particular street in New Jersey, since the story is unfolding there, they would not have any sense of this world. Instead of seeing the world of Evanovich's story, the reader could be inserting images from a Kansas town or a French city, especially if the reader had never been to New Jersey.

Without clues, the reader will default to what they know already and may get an erroneous Setting image. One paragraph was all that was needed to anchor the reader to the world of the characters and make the Setting come alive. Evanovich does not use a lot of Setting in her stories, but makes sure that the reader experiences the world of New Jersey bounty-hunter Stephanie Plum at least once or twice in every story.

Pacing and Setting

If the character is returning to a place that hasn't been described in depth previously, the reader will not be as open to a slower pacing on the revisit so you can describe Setting. The reader has most likely created her own visuals, because a reader needs to see the characters in some context. This is a small but important point, and an error many new writers make.

Beginning writers often:

- wait until it's too late to describe and orient the reader as to place;

- or totally forget that the reader has no idea where the character is in the story, because the location has suddenly moved from a known to a new, unknown location.

If I write, *Joe left his home and went to the city*, the Setting is so vague that it leaves you clueless and frustrated. But if I write, *Joe left his beachside cottage and drove into Lake Forest City, a northern suburb of Seattle*, the addition of a few specifics gives you enough to inhabit the character's world while keeping the main focus on what's happening in the story.

> **NOTE:** You need to sprinkle in clues for the reader to develop a correct Setting image. If you go back and clarify the Setting later, this can pull a reader out of your story because his Setting images did not match yours.

When you move your character from one location in your story to another, it's easy to forget that the reader has never been to this new location and it needs to be quickly anchored.

The following is an example of orienting the reader via Setting when moving a POV character from one location to another. Add more than a hint of Setting only when that new location has an impact on the story.

In this example, the POV character is showing up to a job interview she didn't apply for, but needs. A beginning writer might write something like this:

> **EXAMPLE DRAFT:** I went to the address I was given. The place looked okay so I went in for the interview.

What do you see? A strip mall? A single-story building? What's meant by *okay*? See how much you as the reader have to create because the Setting details are so vague? If this interview and place did not matter to the larger story, you could get away with vagueness. But in this story, the location will become a constant through several books in the series, so the reader needs more information.

Look closely at what the author focuses the reader on while describing this area of New York City.

> The office—or whatever it was—didn't exactly inspire confidence.
> The address was a mostly kept-up building off Amsterdam Avenue,
> seven stories high and nine windows across. Brick and gray stone:
> that looked like the norm in this neighborhood. We weren't
> running with a high-income crowd here. Still, I had seen and
> smelled worse, and the neighborhood looked pretty friendly—lots
> of bodegas and coffee shops, and the kids hanging around looked
> as if they'd stopped there to hang on the way home from school, not
> been there all day waiting for their parole officer to roll by.
> —Laura Anne Gilman, *Hard Magic*

Now let's look closer:

> The office—or whatever it was—didn't exactly inspire confidence.
> [*Wariness is expressed here. The reader gets an emotional feel for
> the area via the POV character's impressions. The reader hasn't seen
> anything yet, but the emotional feel has been established via internal
> dialogue.*] The address was a mostly kept-up building off Amster-
> dam Avenue. [*For those who know New York City, this specific street
> name can say a lot. But those who don't will skim over the specific
> name without context, or assume the POV character is seeing an
> economic state of this particular area of town.*] seven stories high
> and nine windows across. [*Now the reader has a distinct visual and
> physical image.*] Brick and gray stone: that looked like the norm in
> this neighborhood. [*The reader is beginning to be reassured, sub-
> tly, that the POV character can enter this building. That this space
> is the norm means it doesn't stand out as better or worse, and the
> POV character would not be foolish to enter.*] We weren't running
> with a high-income crowd here. Still, I had seen and smelled worse,
> [*Sensory detail (covered in more depth later in this book)—the reader
> doesn't get a specific smell, but is subtly reminded that most of us are
> very aware that the smell of a building or neighborhood can also tell*

us what kind of world the character has entered.] and the neighbor-hood looked pretty friendly—lots of bodegas and coffee shops, and the kids hanging around looked as if they'd stopped there to hang on the way home from school, not been there all day waiting for their parole officer to roll by. [*Here the reader has been refocused from the wariness at the beginning of the paragraph to a sense of comfort—the buildings have not changed, but what the POV character focuses the reader on—kids hanging out after school—creates a different emotion and feel for the buildings, making it understandable why the character now enters the building and doesn't run away screaming.*]

And here's a different example where, in spite of the fact the character is arriving at a place new to her, and new to the reader, the author chose simply to describe and not add much more. Why? Because the reader needs a sense of place in order to explain the events that happen in the story, but not more. Sometimes the author doesn't want the focus shifted into too much detail about the Setting, and that's fine.

You'll find this technique used more often in mysteries, suspense stories, and thrillers where the author wants enough detail to anchor the reader, but not enough to stop the fast-paced momentum or the created tension. Other genre stories can afford more Setting details—historical, women's fiction, SF/fantasy, and literary stories, for example—because the pacing of these genres can be slower. But even in these stories, too much Setting description that adds little to the story can leave readers dead in the water.

In the following passage, a young woman has gone missing after having car trouble near a well-known cemetery.

> Erin knew the road: a narrow strip of pavement that ran a few blocks alongside the sprawling cemetery's high chain-link fence. There was a park on the other side of the road—with a smaller, unfenced, old cemetery for Veterans of Foreign Wars. Only a block away, quaint, charming houses bordered the park, but there was

something remote and slightly foreboding about that little back road—especially at night. Surrounded by so many graves, it was an awfully scary spot to have car problems.

—Kevin O'Brien, *Final Breath*

The last sentence is the reason for the Setting description. If O'Brien had chosen to simply write: *Surrounded by so many graves, it was an awfully scary spot to have car problems,* and skimped on Setting and word choices that created an emotional feel for where the incident happened, the tension and conflict in the story would have been lessened. The reader would have been told the Setting was scary, but not *shown* that it was scary. The story question—what happened to the missing girl?—would not be as strong. But O'Brien did not need to go into other details about this cemetery: that it's the largest in Seattle, the final resting place for Bruce Lee and his son Brandon, and one of the oldest cemeteries in the community. A brief three-sentence description, followed by that key summation line, did its job to show you where the incident happened and why it was plausible that this girl disappeared in this location.

What Not to Do

Some writers will write really long descriptions, such as this one of a tree:

A Utah pine, I suppose. I know it wasn't an alligator. Remembering, I'd say the trunk was about a foot through, but the reason for the tree's importance was a lightning strike that burnt out the core. So the tree was alive on the outside and dead in the middle. The lowest limbs got thick as trunks and the branches went out and up. The shape was perfect for a tree house. After the dead middle trunk was cut off level with the live limbs that is. Scrounged pieces of 2×4 and small offcuts of plywood formed the tree house, which we lined with gunny sacking to make it feel like a real house. Slept in that tree more than once. Now a road goes over where the tree was. I reckon it provided winter fuel for someone's fireplace. The old jailhouse, though, still stands not a hundred yards away.

This description features a lot of details—too many, as you get easily shifted from focusing on a specific tree to several other issues. There are almost too many issues in one paragraph. A character's backstory, how the character feels about the absence of the tree, and a secondary building that's now on the site all can be consistent and compatible images, but there are so many other details about the way the tree looked and what happened to it and in it that the sudden shift to a road and jailhouse seems jarring. The reader's focus is shifted by the use of one or two sentences describing the tree when used as a tree house, sliding into the fact the tree is now gone and instead there's a jail next door. In other words too much information that is not necessary.

Overdescribing can cause story issues that will impact your pacing and frustrate your reader. The most important worldbuilding aspect in the above example is the description of the tree as alive on the outside but dead on the inside. This gives enormous insight to the POV character's world and his relationship to it—we assume the character, too, is alive on the outside, but dead on the inside. No need for details about how the tree fort was built, or the shift to a jailhouse.

Another common Setting detail speed bump:

EXAMPLE: a blue tract home

Here we have too little detail. The author assumes the reader knows what is meant by a tract home, but since tract housing has been around since the seventeenth century, there can be a huge difference between coal-miner homes in an eighteenth-century Cornish town and wooden detached homes created in an American suburb shortly after World War II. Adding a few more specific words will pull your reader deeper into your specific story Setting.

REWRITE: A blue tract home in a 1950s suburb.

A copycat row of brick tract bungalows built for the coal miners, some faded red, others painted blue.

Little wooden box tract houses built for single millworkers or families who couldn't afford more.

NOTE: A few small details can make a huge difference. Don't think that adding Setting means adding paragraphs of details.

EXAMPLE: Tall evergreen

Another example of too little information or vagueness that does not give the reader a strong enough image to either see or experience this tree. What is meant by tall? Does it mean larger than a child, or a two-story house? And since an evergreen tree can technically be any tree that has leaves all year round, one reader might imagine a ponderosa pine, while another sees a blue spruce, and another a live oak—very different-looking trees.

REWRITE: The towering live oak dwarfed the one-story shack built against its trunk. [*The change here gives the reader a clearer idea of the type of tree and its size.*]

The leaning cypress tree once must have stood seventy feet or more, but now looked like a crooked-back elder at half that height. [*The change here gives a specific tree type plus a hint of the tone or feel of the passage.*]

The broad-leafed magnolia once was my height, but now arched taller than my five-foot-seven stretch. [*The change here added a specific tree plus shows the POV character and a hint of his or her backstory.*]

Ignoring Setting details or using vague, nonspecific details as a default mode of writing leaves your reader at a distance from your story. Learning to write with Active Setting will pull your reader in.

Here's an example of Setting that does not need too many details or words because the Setting is not being used to show information about the POV character or to orient the reader into a change in the story's location. The Setting is used to show the reader only one thing.

> Woods surrounded the clearing in which Merlotte's stood, and the edges of the parking lot were mostly gravel. Sam kept it well lit, and the surrealistic glare of the high parking lot lights made everything look strange.
> —Charlaine Harris, *Dead Until Dark*

In the above example, the author wanted to keep the reader focused on the feel and the emotion of the setting, nothing more. Look what would have happened if Harris had chosen to overwrite this Setting.

> **OVERWRITTEN EXAMPLE:** Piney woods with a few wild magnolia trees surrounded the ninety-foot by ninety-foot clearing in which Merlotte's stood, and the edges of the square parking lot were mostly gravel of the light-gray variety, clashing with the red of the Georgia soil. Sam kept the lot well lit with at least six vapor-arc lights high overhead and a spotlight near the front door of the bar. The surrealistic glare of the high parking-lot lights made everything look elongated and warped, like looking into one of those mirrors at carnivals.

See? All this detail shifts the focus away from the mood of the Setting and can slow the story pacing.

A Writer's Guide to Active Setting

don't need that information, if it doesn't improve your story, then leave it out.

Assignment

Part 1

Describe a tree, a house, and a car from your own POV. No right or wrong here, as we're trying to establish your baseline way to use description and Setting. Do this part of the assignment before you look at Part 2. If it helps, think in terms of your story as you describe a tree, a house, and a car.

Part 2

Notice your default way of describing elements of a Setting. Look to see if you write with too much information, not enough information, or with vague word choices.

INTENTION: This is to determine how you most naturally write Setting elements. It's hard to change what we don't understand.

Part 3

Start creating your own library of books where the author creates the world of the story in enough detail that you as a reader feel you are on scene. Notice particularly how these authors use Setting to show characterization and sensory detail. Look at where and how much Setting detail is used.

Recap

- A POV character who feels comfortable or at home in his environment will not see or notice the same details as a character who feels threatened or uncomfortable in that same environment. Be aware of whose POV you are in as you reveal Setting details.

- If your POV character is arriving in a place that hasn't been described in depth earlier in your story, the reader will be more open to slower pacing in order to orient or anchor herself. But only if the Setting matters in some way to the story.
- The more narrative in your story, the slower your pacing, so thread your Setting details in judiciously and intentionally. If the piano in the corner of a room is meant to show the reader the environment of a character, then add the piano. But if a couch and tables are described because they happen to be in a living room, and serve no other function, then refrain from wasting words on their description.
- Be specific in your details versus vague. A Ming vase reveals more than a pretty vase.

02

Using Subjective Setting Detail to Reveal Character

One of the ways that Setting can work harder in your stories is by using it to reveal something about the character viewing the Setting. Instead of stopping the story flow to tell the reader that Joe is a former Special Forces operative, or that Fran loves children, you can show this through their experiences, personalities, and backgrounds.

Here's a generic Setting example:

> The street was a block long with three-story buildings on either side. Most of them brick. One was built out of concrete. All had steps leading down to the sidewalk. Five trees had been planted along the outer curb and several cars were parked along the street.

Pretty bland and nondescript. The reader sees buildings, but not much else. Look what happens when we take Joe and Fran from above and revisit this Setting:

> Joe stood on the corner, with the widest viewpoint of the 400-meter long street running east to west. Buildings squatted, all of uniform height and width, three-stories on either side. Most of them brick, but one of Afghanistan-mud brown concrete. Hide sights for a sniper? Possibly, but nothing stood out. Several areas of vulnerability and strength—the largest areas of view, but no faces

at the windows or along the rooftops. Good. Escape route would be dead ahead or behind, unless he could access the buildings and use the roof. No alleys to create choke points, garbage cans that could contain a bomb, or loose items, backpacks, boxes that could hide an IED. The types and number of vehicles were what he expected on a quiet street, except for the big van that could be surveillance, especially with its out-of-state plates and dark-tinted windows. The one with leaves from one of the scrawny trees fronting the sidewalk littered on its roof, which meant it'd been there for a while.

Do you get a clearer image of not only the street, but of Joe and his background? The reader experiences the street on a deeper level and is right there with Joe, seeing what he's seeing, and learning a lot about him from how he views the Setting.

Let's see how child-loving Fran might see the same street.

The street stretched a block long with the sounds of kids of all ages shouting and laughing, noise that zipped from the three-story buildings on either side. Most of the apartments were brick—the old fashioned-kind of brick that screamed genteel families and industrious lives. One building stood out—being concrete—as if the people who lived there didn't care so much about their surroundings. Steps led down from each home to the cracked sidewalk, filled with chalk drawings and hopscotch squares. Five boxwood trees marched along the outer curb, one with a droopy Happy Birthday balloon snagged in its branches. Several mini-vans and SUVs parked along the street, waiting for the next trip to school or soccer.

So what did you learn about Fran? About what matters in her life? What she wants more of in her world just based on how she subjectively focused on this city block?

NOTE: How the Setting is revealed says a lot about the character.

Joe can't get away from threat assessment whereas Fran is focused on the happy families she sees living there, or the possibility of happy families.

The writer needs to be aware that the relationship between the POV character and the Setting is what allows the reader to see and experience the story on a deeper level.

Showing with Setting

It's important to remember that place can and should be filtered through a specific character's emotions, impressions, viewpoint, and focus—this is how it reveals character and why what one character sees in a Setting can be more important than the Setting itself. Ignoring the powerful use of characterization and Setting decreases the subtext of your story and also decreases the immediacy a character feels in your story world. If your POV character simply walks through a Setting with nothing revealed except that the character is now at a store, on a street, or returning home, you are showing your readers that this Setting doesn't matter that much to the story. So if it does matter, show it!

NOTE: Don't use Setting simply as window dressing.

Let's look at a Setting example that is very active but quickly orients the reader to the fact that the POV character knows this place well, which is an insight into the character's back story. Let's assume though, that the author had scribbled out an early draft.

FIRST DRAFT: I'd known Brooklyn my whole life, especially this part of Brooklyn.

No Setting details here. No sense of place at all, just a plain, telling statement.

SECOND DRAFT: There were different sections of Brooklyn, some old, some newer, all with their own personalities and unwritten rules.

Here there's a stronger sense that the character knows and understands the Setting. But a reader who is unfamiliar with Brooklyn, or which area of Brooklyn is being used, is forced to either create his own images, or become restless while waiting to find out why it's important to understand where the events are unfolding.

If the Setting does not add to the scene, if it's not important to the story, then either the first or second drafts above could work. But let's see how the author, Jonathan Lethem, brought the Setting, and thus the story, alive with his brief but powerful passage.

> Minna's Court Street was the old Brooklyn, a placid ageless surface alive underneath with talk, with deals and casual insults, a neighborhood political machine with pizzeria and butcher-shop bosses and unwritten rules everywhere. All was talk except for what mattered most, which were unspoken understandings.
>
> —Jonathan Lethem, *Motherless Brooklyn*

The author uses a combination of telling—*was old Brooklyn, a placid ageless surface alive underneath with talk, with deals and casual insults*—and showing—*Minna's Court Street, a neighborhood, pizzeria and butcher-shop*—that creates a stronger sense that the events about to unfold in the story could happen only here. The reader has enough details to paint an image of this street, in this particular city, without the story skidding to a halt with details that are unimportant.

NOTE: In a novel, and in real life, what an individual focuses on reveals a lot about that character's state of mind, history, personality, and more.

Right Information/Right Signals

Don't confuse the reader. They are coming to your Setting with very little context, so they are trying to visualize the *who*, *where*, and *when* of the location and *how* it feeds into your story. So you might go back and edit to make sure you're:

- Sharing the right information and sending the right signals for that character. Fran would not think of offensive and defensive positions, and Joe would not notice chalk drawings unless they constituted a threat.
- Filtering the Setting through the experience, emotion, and mindset of one character at a time.
- Not stopping the story flow to show place, or details of a place, unless that place reveals something that's important to know about the characters.

NOTE: Adding Setting description is not necessarily an intrusion on the page if it is an extension of the character's communication. This is important to realize if your first drafts are heavy on showing characters via their dialogue or movement.

Revealing Character Through Setting

> She glanced toward the windows of her office, which were barred and always shaded. The glare of a bright winter's day peeked around the edges of old-fashioned blinds.
>
> —Laura Lippman, *In A Strange City*

Look at the details Lippman uses to reveal about her mystery series protagonist, Tess Monaghan, who has a complicated relationship with her life and her world. Examine the specific word choices made, not through telling but through showing.

> She glanced toward the windows of her office, [*Up to this point the character is simply doing what any person can do in any office on any given day. There's no sense of place or character.*] which were barred and always shaded. [*These are specific, telling details. This is not the Setting of someone connected to her world outside, wanting to see its pulse, watching it unfold daily. No, this is a person barricaded, by choice, on a consistent basis. This office is her fortress, which reveals*

so much.] The glare of a bright winter's day [*Again, a very revealing word choice here. In the northern areas of the United States, or any country that deals with lower light levels in the winter, if you change the relationship the character has with the quality or quantity of light you will show very different personalities: the straining warmth of a winter's day; the soft, blue white of a winter's day; the clear spotlight of a winter's day. These are all very different descriptions that can be used to show different personalities.*] peeked around the edges of old-fashioned blinds. [*Again, not any kind of blinds but old-fashioned ones. This leaves the detail up to the reader to translate what she sees—dusty, wide shades or skinny, mass-produced plastic slats from the 1980s. It's not important to know exactly what kind of shades they are, but it is important to know this character hides behind the shades, keeping them intentionally closed as protection and, perhaps, avoidance. A lot is revealed as a result of two very specific, very intentional sentences about Setting.*]

This next example comes from the opening pages of a mystery novel in the POV of the protagonist, First Commissaire Adamsberg. We're inside his skin, experiencing his memories as he gives readers a sense of who he is, based on where he came from. Let's see how the author, Fred Vargas, does that.

> As a child, Jean-Baptiste Adamsberg had run around barefoot in the stony foothills of the Pyrenees. He had lived and slept there, and later, after becoming a policeman, he had been obliged to work on murders committed there, murders in the stone-built villages, murders on the rocky paths. He knew by heart the sounds of pebbles underfoot and the mountain's way of gripping and clutching you to its heart like a muscular old man.
> —Fred Vargas, *The Chalk Circle Man*

If we dissect this example, we can see why it works so well.

> As a child, Jean-Baptiste Adamsberg had run around barefoot in the stony foothills of the Pyrenees. [*Straight telling at this point.*

The reader is given a basic statement of fact and, unless the reader is familiar with the Pyrenees, this sentence doesn't pull them deeper into the story. It's the same as someone introducing a stranger to you and simply stating that they come from a town or area you know little about.] He had lived and slept there, [*Small, fresh way of starting to show the reader that this place may have shaped this man. If the author had said only—he lived there—and moved on, there would not be that small emphatic beat that says pay attention, this matters.]* and later, after becoming a policeman, [*Another statement of fact.]* he had been obliged to work on murders committed there, murders in the stone-built villages, murders on the rocky paths. [*Here is the double-beat that if eliminated would decrease the imagery of where this man was shaped. The adjectives stone-built and rocky, are deliberately used to build to the next sentence and make the reader wonder about this character who was so shaped by his early environment.]* He knew by heart the sounds of pebbles underfoot [*Audio detail here that allows the reader to be this character as a child, feel what he felt, which creates a stronger image of the individual via specific Setting details.]* and the mountain's way of gripping and clutching you to its heart like a muscular old man. [*This last line is almost poetical and reveals that this man has some depth, thinking of his childhood in this way. So the reader now has a hint of backstory and a stronger sense that this character is still very much a product shaped by this specific Setting.]*

If the author had stopped with *obliged to work on murders committed there*, the reader would be held at arm's length, waiting to be intrigued about this man. He'd be told but not shown. But the author is building to the showing elements, step-by-step; the personality of the man is being revealed. The phrases *murders in the stone-built villages* and *murders on the rocky paths* bring to mind the imagery of rocks and stones which helps define to the reader the type of man this Inspector is—a man raised in a harsh environment and a world away from the streets of Paris where he is now assigned. This insight in turn raises questions about him. Is he flinty? Isolated? A hard loner? When questions such as these are raised, a reader becomes intrigued enough to keep reading, even just a little more, to discover the answers. Then the author can drop the most revealing line—*He knew by heart the sounds of pebbles underfoot and the mountain's way of gripping and clutching you to its heart like a muscular old man.* There's no explanation as to whether this was a good thing or not, but it reveals a lot about the man, the one who thinks in these terms about where he grew up, and where he no longer lives.

Here's the beginning of a Setting passage from a Nancy Pickard mystery. This novel is part of a series, so the author chooses to reveal character via Setting rather than simply repeat what readers of the series may have already learned. You discover so much about this couple by what the POV character sees just by looking around her own living room.

> Our furniture didn't match, at least not in theory, but it fit together perfectly in practice. We'd used my favorite clear, bright colors— yellows, oranges, reds—and mixed them with his favorite deep brown wood tones, so the house had an autumnal atmosphere all year long, kind of crisp and cheerful and cozy all at once. There were always books and magazines littering the rooms like scattered leaves, and often a week's worth of newspapers trailing from the kitchen to our bedroom upstairs and the bathrooms down to the living room and finally into recycling. And books, so many books it looked as if a convention of librarians had dropped by with armloads and joyously tossed it all up in the air and dumped everything, leaving us to sort through the detritus on our deliciously erratic quest for wisdom.
>
> —Nancy Pickard, *Confession*

The passage continues on, but serves so well in revealing who these characters are. It gives the reader a broader understanding of who they are, as a couple and individually, by what they surround themselves with— these two are comfortable with themselves, casual, and intelligent.

What if Pickard chose to tell, not show? What if she wrote:

> Our home reflects the fact we are intelligent people comfortable
> with our lives and who we are.

NOTE: Straight telling does not reveal half as much as showing does.

Since this novel is part of a series, Pickard does not necessarily need to describe this room in this much detail in later novels because loyal readers will remember this room. In another book the author could choose to highlight a different room in the house—the kitchen, bedroom, or even the garage—so readers new to the series, as well as the series regulars, can experience this home on a deeper level. By seeing these characters in their environment, the reader feels more a part of the world of the story.

I'm not saying that in every story you want this much Setting description for every character, or that you have to reveal character every time, but I do want you to think in terms of how this one specific POV character relates to this Setting versus a different character. It's a great place to open up opportunities to reveal your character to the reader in different ways.

In this next example from a historical novel set in the 1920s, a young woman who has set off a recent scandal has been forced to face the consequences—banishment to Africa for a suitable period of time until the furor dies down. It's clear up to this point in the story that while she is not opposed to seeing Africa, she also feels unjustly punished for nothing more than an indiscretion. She loves Paris and feels that she will return as soon as possible. The author could simply tell the reader:

> **ROUGH DRAFT:** The day I left Paris I knew I would be returning
> as soon as possible.

This is how newer writers might approach the departure scene, instead of digging a little bit deeper into the POV of the character to reveal her relationship with this city of her heart.

> Paris had dressed in her best to see us off. A warm spring sun peeked through the pearl-grey skirts of early morning fog. And a light breeze stirred the new leaves on the Champs-Elysees as if waving fare well.
>
> —Deanna Raybourn, *A Spear of Summer Grass*

What happens if we take out the descriptive words and details from the above example?

> Paris saw us off. It was spring on the Champs-Elysees.

Fairly blah with no sense of a love affair with this city or any interaction with this location. If that was the case, the above sentence might work, but part of the conflict built into this story is the fact that this character loves Paris and does not want to leave. The author used the opportunity to drive that point home, not by direct telling, but by showing the character's response to her departure.

What if the character was glad she was leaving Paris?

> Paris spit snow and sleet to see us off. Weak sunlight did little to warm the damp grey facades, hunkered down and braced for more cold. And a breeze rattled the bare branches on the Champs-Elysees as if hurrying us along on our departure.

OR:

> Paris had dressed in her aristocratic snobbishness to see us off. Tepid sunlight fell across the damp sidewalks and row upon row of stone buildings, their shutters drawn and blank. A Seine-scented breeze wafted from the river beyond the Champs-Elysees as if taunting us to return.

Three very different Settings create three very different insights as to whom the POV character is and how she feels about leaving Paris.

NOTE: Make sure your details truly reflect the viewpoint of the character experiencing the Setting, if it matters to the story.

Let's examine another example of characterization shown through Setting.

> "Out of the way, please. Sheriff investigator. Come on now. Out."
>
> Merci Rayburn ducked under the ribbon and continued down the walk. Her heart was beating fast and her senses were jacked up high, registering all at once the cars hissing along Coast Highway to her left, waves breaking on the other side of the building, the citizens murmuring behind her, the moon hanging low over the eastern hills, the smell of ocean and exhaust, the night air cool against her cheeks, the walkway slats bending under her duty boots. She figured a place like this, ocean front in San Clemente, would run you two grand a month and you still got termites in your walkway and spider webs high in the porch corners.
>
> —T. Jefferson Parker, *Red Light*

This one-paragraph description that opens the story shows a lot about the character by how she looks at the Setting. The reader is not introduced to the crime scene as a laundry list of narrative description—building, location, time of day. Instead, while actively moving the story forward, the author threads all of this information through the character's description of the Setting in such a subtle way that the reader is pulled deeper into the story and skin of the POV character.

We learn that Merci can multi-task and take in many different details at once, a good characteristic for an investigator to have. Therefore the author can slip in other important details later in the story without the reader feeling that it's strange for Merci to notice. The paragraph also lets us know that Merci covers her uncomfortable emotions with snarky thoughts—*a place like this, ocean front in San Clemente, would run you two grand a month and you still got termites in your walkway and spider webs high in the porch corners*. Later, if Merci does this again, the reader can assume she's uncomfortable in some way.

In the next example, the author uses Setting description to show the thought process of the POV character and where he's coming from while filtering in insights about a secondary character. The POV character, Joe Pike, has been assigned to protect the life of a spoiled rich girl. Two attempts have already been made on her life, the latest one while she's been in Pike's custody, so he's now taking charge of the situation by moving her to a new location (remember when you shift your characters to a new location, you shift your readers, and they need to be anchored all over again).

Let's assume Robert Crais, the author, wrote a rough draft first:

> **ROUGH DRAFT:** Joe and the girl arrived at the new location. She didn't look happy about the place, but it looked like it'd work for him.

Do you see why the POV character sees her displeasure or why he makes the judgment call? Not really. You're told, which holds you at arm's length from the story until something else happens.

Look at how the author shows what Joe Pike reveals about himself, and about his impressions of the girl, in this one paragraph of Setting.

> The girl was moody getting out of the car, making a sour face to let him know she hated the shabby house and sun-scorched street smelling of chili and epazote. To him, this anonymous house would serve. He searched the surrounding houses for threats as he waited for her, clearing the area the way another man might clear his throat. He felt obvious wearing the long-sleeved shirt. The Los Angeles sun was too hot for the sleeves, but he had little choice. He moved carefully to hide what was under the shirt.
>
> She said, "People who live in houses like this have deformed children. I can't stay here."
>
> —Robert Crais, *The Watchman*

We get a sense of Joe Pike looking for threats and assessing safety issues: he's not here because the neighborhood is safe, but because he can keep her safe here. The house is anonymous. He doesn't think about the people in the houses or the paint job or anything but security. This also shows a lot about the intrinsic differences between him and the girl he's guarding by her response to the Setting and how he sees her response. There's a lot going on in one paragraph, but the forward momentum of the story never slows down.

Let's look at another example, this time from an author who is always good to study for her ability to make every word do double duty. In this description we're about a third of the way into the story, and the POV character is looking for a tenuous lead on her missing ex-sister-in-law.

First, let's look at this as if the author was writing from first draft to finished version.

> **NOTE:** Since we are using the work of published authors as examples, the rough first draft is imagined. Of course there's no telling what the author initially wrote or how many drafts he used to get to the final product. What you should look at are the possibilities you can apply to your own work if you currently lack Setting detail.

> **FIRST DRAFT:** I drove my vehicle into the hills to my sister-in-law's house.

Bland. No sense of location. All the writer did was get the character from point A to point B. Sometimes an author simply needs a transition sentence or two to move a character through time and space. But often the writer is missing a rich treasure trove of showing more, or showing with telling, that can make a story so much richer if she wrote with intention.

> **SECOND DRAFT:** I drove my rig into the hills above Santa Barbara, and when I arrived at my sister-in-law's place, I stopped and checked it out.

A little better. Now the reader knows where the POV character is, but we're not experiencing any of what that character is experiencing or the interaction she's having with what she's seeing.

Now see if you can tell what the POV character thinks about her ex-sister-in-law by what she observes of the surroundings and interior of the woman's cabin.

> The sun was flaring red in the west when I drove my white Explorer up a gully toward Tabitha's house, past sandstone boulders and gray-green brush. The air smelled thick with mustard and eucalyptus. The view of the city, two thousand feet below, was spectacular. Santa Barbara lay like a velvet sash between the mountains and the Pacific, smooth and glimmering.
>
> The house itself looked neglected. Faded gray paint curled from the wood siding, and weeds spread across the lawn, humped and matted, like an overgrown beard. When no one answered my knock, I looked in the front window. The living room held some thrift-shop chairs and a work table covered with pens, pencils, and drawings. In the dingy kitchen, shopping bags bulged with cans of creamed corn and SPAM. Was that what she cooked for Brian? No wonder he had requested sea duty.
>
> —Meg Gardiner, *China Lake*

Notice the author uses contrast between the city of Santa Barbara, known to be one of the most exclusive of Southern California's coastal towns (also known for its red-tiled roofs which creates the red of the red-sash imagery), and the area surrounding the home, to show the POV character's feelings as she enters her sister-in-law's world. Gardiner also doesn't leave the reader to guess the POV character's impressions or emotions surrounding her ex-sister-in-law, choosing words such as *neglected, faded, humped, matted, thrift shop,* and *dingy* to describe her living space. She even names the specific food that's visible—*creamed corn and SPAM.*

One last point to notice is that Gardiner doesn't stop the story to give a description; she filters in sensory details and movement—*driving, looking*—with internalization (her internal thought process). This is a powerful use of description that places the reader in the Setting and gives insights into the POV character and the ex-sister-in-law.

> **NOTE:** Notice the specific word choice of velvet—a tactile, luxurious, even glamorous fabric used to contrast with the rough and decidedly unglamorous house. A clever use of the sense of touch for something we wouldn't ordinarily think of touching (the ocean, the city, the lawn, the house siding).

Contrast in Setting

Using Setting to contrast one character's world with another character's can power up characterization by threading in conflict at the same time. In the next example, from a paranormal romance series, the author uses contrast in characterization to make it clear that the hero in the story comes from a radically different environment than the rich, upper-crust heroine. This passage describes what the heroine sees and experiences when she enters a favored place frequented by the hero. The reader already knows from the hero's POV that he feels out of her league, so let's see how the author brings home that point by seeing his environment from her POV.

> Mike's gym was a man's world, baby. Place smelled like an armpit, had walls that were prison-worthy, and was hung with faded pictures of Arnold from back in the eighties.
> —J.R. Ward, *Crave*

Two succinct sentences and the reader learns more about the hero, by the place he feels most comfortable in, and about the heroine, who does not belong in this environment and has very different feelings based on what she focuses on. Notice how the author uses the power of three to bring home the points she wants to make. A novice writer might stop with:

INITIAL DRAFT: Mike's gym was a man's world.

But the author added three more beats to bring home her points:

> Place smelled like an armpit, [*Beat one—a sensory detail that pulls the reader into the odor of the gym.*] had walls that were prison-worthy, [*Second beat—a visual here that is less about the colors of the walls and more about the message that the men who hung out here, including the hero, could feel right at home in a prison.*] and was hung with faded pictures of Arnold from back in the eighties. [*Third beat—very specific detail; using a pop-culture icon associated with bodybuilding makes this place real, not generic, and lets the reader step into the scene while understanding both characters just a little bit more.*]

The next example is a fascinating passage—it's a little long, which impacts the pacing of the story, but reveals so much about the protagonist Lisbeth Salander. In the first section, the author shows almost a full page of Salander's decision-making process as she contrasts her current apartment with where she might like to live. Notice what this decision-making process reveals about her character.

> She had never thought about an alternative to the 500 square foot in Lundagatan, where she had spent her childhood. Through her trustee at the time, the lawyer Holger Palmgren, she had been granted permission of the apartment when she turned eighteen. She plopped down on the lumpy sofa in her combination office/living room and began to think.
>
> The apartment on Lundagatan looked into a courtyard. It was cramped and not the least bit comfortable. The view from her bedroom was a firewall on a gable façade. The view from the kitchen was of the back of the building facing the street and the entrance to the basement storage area. She could see a streetlight from her living room, and a few branches of a birch tree.
>
> The first requirement of her new home was that it should have some sort of view.

She did not have a balcony, and had always envied well-to-do neighbors higher up in the building who spent warm days with a cold beer under an awning on theirs. The second requirement was that her new home would have a balcony.

What should the apartment look like? She thought about Blomkvist's apartment—700 square feet in one open space in a converted loft on Bellmansgatan with views of City Hall and the locks at Slussen. She liked it there. She wanted to have a pleasant, sparsely furnished apartment that was easy to take care of. That was the third point on her list of requirements.

For years she had lived in cramped spaces. Her kitchen was a mere 100 square feet, with room for only a tiny table and two chairs. Her living room was 200 square feet. The bedroom was 120. Her fourth requirement was that the new apartment should have plenty of space and closets. She wanted to have a proper office and a big bedroom where she could spread herself out.

Her bathroom was a windowless cubbyhole with square cement slabs on the floor, an awkward half bath, and plastic wallpaper that never got really clean no matter how hard she scrubbed it. She wanted a washing machine in the apartment and not down in some basement. She wanted to have tiles and a big bath. She wanted the bathroom to smell fresh, and she wanted to be able to open a window.
—Stieg Larsson, *The Girl Who Played With Fire*

As I indicated, this was a long passage, occurring in the first one hundred pages, but the author consciously slowed the reading experience so that the reader could see how this young woman, Salander, was metamorphosing. He showed where Salander was coming from to highlight where she was going. She encountered obstacles while finding a new place, but she persevered—which showed more characterization—and managed to acquire a new apartment. Later the author spends several more pages showing Salander making quite an extensive trip through IKEA to purchase new furniture to replace her marginal leftovers. But the reader sees very little of the new apartment, except that it does have a view and she bought furniture for a spare bedroom. We're shown only what matters to Salander—that her apartment is large enough to have a spare room, all the furniture is new, and that's about it.

Later in the same story, five-hundred pages later, another character, Mikael Blomkvist, is asked to describe the protagonist's sofa as a means of verifying that he really did know her, because the protagonist has a well-earned reputation of guarding her privacy, which includes her home space, to an extreme degree.

> On the occasions I visited her she had a worn-out, extremely ugly piece of furniture with a certain curiosity value. I would guess it's from the early fifties. It has two shapeless cushions covered in brown cloth with a yellow pattern of sorts on it. The cloth is torn in several places and the stuffing was coming out when I saw it last.
> —Stieg Larsson, *The Girl Who Played With Fire*

Doesn't this description of one piece of furniture give you a unique perspective on who Salander is? The use of specific Setting details over the course of a book is used to symbolize change—the change in who Salander is from an earlier book and the start of the current story, what she values—or not. Setting reveals in small stages the growth of this character from totally isolated to one willing to live in a different way.

Later, Blomkvist has finally found Salander's current apartment. Here's his description:

> Blomkvist was standing at that moment by a window looking out at a magnificent view that stretched far from Gamla Stan towards Saltsjon. He felt numb. There was a kitchen off the hall to the right of the front door. Then there was a living room, an office, a bedroom, and even a guest room that seemed not to have been used. The mattress was still in its plastic wrapper and there were no sheets. All the furniture was brand-new, straight from IKEA.
> What floored Blomkvist was that Salander had bought the pied-a-terre that had belonged to Percy Barnevik, a captain of industry.

The apartment was about 3,800 square feet and worth twenty-five million kroner.

Blomkvist wandered through deserted, almost eerily empty corridors and rooms with patterned parquet floors of different kinds of woods, and Tricia Guild wallpaper of the type that Berger had once coveted. At the center of the apartment was a wonderfully bright living room with an open fireplace, but Salander seemed never to have had a fire. There was an enormous balcony with a fantastic view. There was a laundry room, a sauna, a gym, storage rooms and a bathroom with a king-size bath. There was even a wine cellar, which was empty except for an unopened bottle of Quinta do Noval port National! –from 1976. Blomkvist struggled to imagine Salander with a glass of port in her hand. An elegant card indicated that it had been a moving-in present from the estate agent.

The kitchen contained all manner of equipment, with a shiny French gourmet stove with a gas oven as the focus. Blomkvist had never before set eyes on a Cornue Chateau 120. Salander probably used it for boiling tea.

[*The description goes on for another page until the author wraps up with the following paragraphs.*]

The arrangement was all out of proportion. Salander had stolen several billion kroner and bought herself an apartment with space for an entire court. But she only needed the three rooms she had furnished. The other eighteen rooms were empty.

Blomkvist ended his tour in her office. There were no flowers anywhere. There were no paintings or even posters on the wall. There were no rugs or wall hangings. He could not see a single decorative bowl, candlestick, or even a knick-knack that had been saved for sentimental reasons.

Blomkvist felt as if someone were squeezing his heart. He felt that he had to find Salander and hold her close.

She would probably bite him if he tried.

—Stieg Larsson, *The Girl Who Played With Fire*

I'm not advocating using so many words to describe the personal space of every character, or even using such long descriptions of Setting in every story, but in this 724-page novel, the author chooses to show much of Salander's personality via her living space, and it works.

The reader sees only three rooms, and only the furnishings of those rooms, because that's what matters to Salander. These rooms make her appear as if her life is full and positively changing. But because we are able to get a different perspective on Salander's private space, from another character, Blomkvist, it allows the reader to see her in a very different light and to feel, much like Blomkvist feels, that this young woman is very isolated and alone. By allocating enough words in his descriptions, Larsson brings home the shock of the contrast of those descriptions.

Here's another short passage from a science fiction story. The author's intention is not to contrast personal space as Larsson did in the last example, but to move the character from a public space to her private space (mostly private as she shares it with another character called March). The author also gives the readers a sense that they are really on a ship hurtling through space. If Ann Aguirre, the author, wrote a rough-draft version, it might have been something like this:

> **ROUGH DRAFT:** I left the cockpit to go to my sleeping area, which I share with March. It's not much but it works.

Doesn't do a lot to pull you into this story's world, does it? So let's see how Aguirre ratchets up her worldbuilding, which makes it easier to see the rest of the ship based on this one private space:

> With a jaunty wave, I leave the cockpit and head to my quarters. I share space with March. Despite cohabitation, it's still an austere environment: plain berth, terminal, lighting fortified with solar stimulators to compensate for lack of nutrient D3 if you spend too much time on board.
>
> —Ann Aguirre, *Killbox*

One sentence of details is all that is needed to go from bland to something very different. Does it matter whether we know what all the details mean? Not really. What we get is a stronger sense of the larger world of the story without miring the pacing.

Here's another example from mystery author Walter Mosley. The POV character, Easy Rawlins, has tracked down a lead on a missing person he is seeking. Instead of describing his impressions of the missing person directly, Mosley reveals the character through what he sees of the man's home environment.

> It was a studio apartment. A Murphy bed had been pulled down from the wall. It was unmade and jumbled with dirty clothes and dishes. A black-and-white portable TV with bent-up rabbit-ear antennas sat on a maple chair at the foot of the bed. There was no sofa, but three big chairs, upholstered with green carpeting, were set in a circle facing each other at the center of the room.
>
> The room smelled strongly of perfumes and body odors. This scent of sex and sensuality was off-putting on a Saturday afternoon.
>
> —Walter Mosley, *Cinnamon Kiss*

What if Mosley had decided to shortchange the reader here and go for a more abbreviated room description?

> **ROUGH DRAFT:** It was a messy studio apartment. The man must have been a low-life loser to live in such a place. Plus it stunk.

Sometimes that's all a reader needs, but that is telling, not showing. With a few more lines of Setting, the author brings the reader deeper into the missing man's character by showing who he is.

Let's look at the approach of another mystery author, Sara Paretsky, whose novels about private investigator V.I. Warshawski are classics for understanding the power of Setting in an ongoing series. Here the author reveals a great deal about a secondary character, a man who might have known something about an insurance scam the character may be involved in. Look at the specific details the protagonist hones in on when visiting this man's office for the first time. See how long it takes you to determine the financial status, success, and even the personality of the man by what Warshawski notes.

> Midway Insurance was wedged between a dentist and a gynecologist. The black letters on the door, telling me they insured life, home, and auto, had been there a long time: part of the H in Home had peeled away, so that it looked like Midway insured nome.
> —Sara Paretsky, *Total Recall*

And a paragraph or two later:

> Four large filing cabinets took up most of the remaining space. A curling poster of the Chinese national table-tennis team provided the only decorations. A large pot hung from a chain above the window but the plant within had withered down to a few drying leaves.
> —Sara Paretsky, *Total Recall*

Is this man up and coming in his chosen field? Comfortably well off? On his way down? Never once does the author come out and tell the reader this man had financial motives for the insurance crime, didn't care a whit about his business, or was one step away from possible bankruptcy. She didn't have to, as she showed the reader through two well-crafted and specific detail-loaded paragraphs.

> **NOTE:** The important element to remember is that place can and should be filtered through a specific character's emotions, impressions, viewpoint, and focus. How one character sees a Setting can be more important than the Setting itself.

Ignoring the powerful use of characterization and Setting can decrease the subtext of your story and diminish the potential for a reader to experience your story world.

What Not to Do

- Refrain from shifting POV in the middle of a Setting description.
- Don't use your author POV instead of your character's POV.
- Avoid having multiple characters notice the same Setting details in the same way.
- Don't forget that what you, as the author, focus on via character sends a message to the reader to pay attention: this information will matter later in the story. If the Setting doesn't, or the detail won't, matter, do not spend too many words describing it.
- Don't allocate words on a page to describe Setting if that Setting doesn't matter to your story.
- Avoid confusing your reader with vague (or no) information as to where a character is in a story.
- Don't be inconsistent in your word choices to describe a Setting. If your POV character loves a Setting, let your word choices show that. If they hate it or are indifferent or wary, let your word choices reveal that.

Assignment

If you are not currently working on a manuscript or feel more comfortable working on a generic situation, try Part 1 of this assignment. If you have a WIP (Work In Progress), feel free to try Part 2. Do whichever part works for you in order to understand the power of Setting to show characterization.

Part 1

Choose a room in your home. Look for a more private or personal room—a bedroom, writing area, kitchen—versus a public space—living room, bathroom. This particular room should be anywhere you'd feel comfortable having strangers come in and walk through.

Now describe this room in two to four sentences maximum from the following POVs:

- yours
- an acquaintance or relative you think may disapprove of you or your life choices
- your POV (first or third person) looking at a stranger's place while giving an impression of yourself to the reader

Again, only two to four sentences max. What do you focus on? What do they focus on? What words do you choose to describe your space? What are their word choices that show you are in a different POV? What do your word choices reveal about the character viewing the room and the character that lives in the room?

Part 2

Choose a Setting description of less than a paragraph from your story. In a maximum of two to four sentences, show this Setting through the following POVs, even if you do not use all three in your manuscript:

- the protagonist's POV
- a secondary character's POV, especially one who is very different from the protagonist
- your protagonist's POV again, but this time giving an impression of another character by describing that character's relationship with the protagonist's Setting

Again, only two to four sentences maximum. What does the protagonist focus on? What does the secondary character (antagonist, villain, or a throwaway character) focus on? What are his choices to describe the Setting? How do these word choices change the feel of the Setting and what the reader sees?

INTENTION: The purpose of this exercise is to start to show you the power of POV as it relates to Setting. Change the POV, and though the Setting might remain the same, the impressions the reader receives of that Setting can vary wildly.

> **NOTE:** If those impressions don't change while doing the above assignment, or they don't change in your manuscript when you shift POV, then you are most likely showing the Setting through your own POV, as opposed to that of your characters.

Recap

Remember that place can and should be filtered through a specific character's emotions, impressions, viewpoint, and focus. How one character sees a Setting can be more important than the Setting itself.

Do not stop or slow your story's flow to show a Setting or details of a Setting, unless that Setting reveals something important about the story or characters.

Consider showing the same setting through two different characters to reveal information about the POV character or information about another character that they may not know about themselves. For example, if a young woman thinks of herself as independent and self-contained, and the reader is shown from her personal space how she has saved mementos of her childhood or of the people who have cared for her in the past, you are showing the reader something about the character that she herself does not realize.

03

Using Sensory Detail to Enhance Setting

Sensory detail is one of the most underrated tools in a writer's toolbox and can make a world of difference in creating novels that stand out in a reader's mind. Not every Setting needs all five senses described in detail—that approach is overkill and can have a major impact on your story pacing, not to mention overwhelming the reader with information. But when introducing the reader to a character, changing the location of the story, or focusing a reader on a place that's going to play a larger role in the story, then by all means dig deeper to create a strong Setting image. And a key way to do this is via sensory details.

How to Use Sensory Detail in Your Novel

Use sensory details in your Setting when you first change a location, open a chapter, or to indicate a shift in the emotional state of the POV character. Think in terms of which sensory details a POV character would notice at that particular time. If you change the time and emotional state of the POV character, then there should be a difference in which sensory details the character notices. An example might be listening to specific music at the opening of the scene. What can be soft and relaxing at the beginning of the scene can be lonely and low-energy at the end. Have you ever entered a favorite store and found the music upbeat and fun, only to discover that the person with you finds the same music annoying and dated? Each person's description of the music would create a different feel for a reader about the store's Setting.

Understanding Texture

Texture is often overlooked in a story but it can act as a metaphor rich in symbolism for the POV character. One character standing in an Iowa cornfield, feeling the wind and the sun enveloping her, feels nurtured and can feel the richness of the soil and the expanse of the Setting. Another character in the same Setting can feel the dirt coating his tongue, the sun beating down on him, drying his skin and sucking the life out of him with its relentless sameness.

Think of the feel of different times of the day during different seasons. I moved from a four-season climate to a two-season climate and am still waiting for certain sensory cues as to what season it is. Daily temperatures alone don't tell me.

But think beyond simple hot, warm, cold. One character who is very athletic or runs on a warmer core body temperature (many men, especially young men, can fall into this category) may find a cool environment just to his liking, whereas another character in the same environment is shivering. (I'm always that other character!) Also think of other tactile experiences—what does wind feel like? Or fog? Or dry dust in the air versus humidity?

Look how Laurell K. Hamilton uses the texture of air to open chapter thirty-seven in her novel. Keep in mind the reader is deep into the story here, but the author doesn't miss an opportunity to pull the reader in deeper in order to feel the scene and the change of location and emotion by focusing on key sensory details:

> Early-morning light lay heavy and golden on the street outside. The air was cool and misty. You couldn't see the river from here,

but you could feel it; that sense of water on the air that made every breath fresher, cleaner.

—Laurell K. Hamilton, *Circus of the Damned*

Can you smell the air in Hamilton's description? Feel it brush against your own skin? The reader is given momentary breathing space before the POV character is thrust into deeper trouble in the story. This two-sentence chapter opening helps create the emotional roller coaster that starts here, in a lovely awareness of the Setting, to what comes next, which is just the opposite.

Now we're shifting to a different genre, a thriller novel from Frank Wilem. Like many thrillers, this story occurs in many locations throughout the world. That's one of the intriguing elements of thrillers—their exotic locales—along with their gritty realism. But the story must be kept tense and fast-paced. That's a lot for a writer to juggle, so let's look closely at how Wilem achieves just that. Before we jump to his final draft, let's assume he wrote an initial draft to get a feel for exactly what he wanted to impart to the reader.

> **FIRST DRAFT:** Dean was located on a discarded fishing trawler, waiting for his mission to commence.

Not much at all here to make the reader feel they are hunkered down on a rusty trawler. At this point the reader knows they are in Uzbekistan and that Dean was asleep on this trawler and awakened by the sounds of a local scavenger working nearby. So there are lots of possibilities to not only compel a reader to keep reading, but to anchor them deeply into this Setting. Let's see how Wilem approached the challenge:

> A bead of sweat fell from his nose as he eased away from the port-hole and slid down onto the hard steel floor. He twisted the cap off his canteen and drained a quarter of it to replace the fluids the arid desert sucked from his body. The smell of rotted fish, old diesel fuel, and the Aral Sea filled his nostrils. Flecks of paint stained

brown-red clung to the backs of his arms and the legs of his desert-camouflaged fatigues where they had rested on the deck.

—Frank Wilem, *The Aral*

Let's pull these three Setting sentences apart to see why they are working so hard:

A bead of sweat fell from his nose [*Tactile detail the reader can feel with the character.*] as he eased away from the porthole [*Reminder that he's still on the abandoned boat.*] and slid down onto the hard steel floor. [*Another tactile detail—it's not just metal but steel, and hard at that.*] He twisted the cap off his canteen and drained a quarter of it to replace the fluids the arid desert sucked from his body. [*Here, instead of simply showing the character drinking, the author brings the Setting back in so the reader can feel what being in this type of environment means.*] The smell of rotted fish, [*He did not need to describe what type of fish here—by focusing only on the scent, anyone who has ever smelled decaying fish knows what he's smelling.*] old diesel fuel, [*Another specific detail that enhances the image of the abandoned fishing trawler.*] and the Aral Sea filled his nostrils. [*Here he did not have to say salty brine, putrid stench, or anything else. By not adding in a clarifying description with the words Aral Sea, the author implies it too stinks or smells very, very bad, which, as the reader keeps reading, is the whole point of this story.*] Flecks of paint stained brown-red [*And here the author did not stop with just the feel and visual of paint flecks, but makes a very graphic image clear by describing them as brown-red, which also happens to be the color of dried blood.*] clung to the backs of his arms and the legs of his desert-camouflaged fatigues [*And this detail, though not specifically about the Setting, hints that this man might be military, or ex-military, which raises questions about who he is and why is he here.*] where they had rested on the deck.

Are you, as a reader, in the POV of the character in this passage? Can you feel the heat, inhale the specific scents, see the paint flecks? This is the type of gritty realism readers of this genre love. They want to be in the skin of the character, out on the edge of nowhere, facing danger and discomfort for the sake of a larger good.

The next example clearly anchors the reader in the world of Victorian England through the author's strategic use of sensory details. This is from the opening of a scene moving the protagonist from the city of London to a smaller community on the outskirts that, in the 1800s, was still rural. The character's intention is to interview a possible witness who can shed light on a gruesome murder that occurred at one of the city's most well-known hospitals. The author's first draft might have been something like this:

> **FIRST DRAFT:** William Monk decided to walk the distance between the hospital and the residence of a woman who could shed some light on the murder victim's past.

The above keeps the focus on the murder, but does not pull the reader into the Victorian time period. And there are no sensory details.

> **SECOND DRAFT:** The day was hot and the route crowded as William Monk left the hospital to discover more clues.

Technically there's a sense of the weather, but it's so generic as to be all but invisible. The reader isn't in the skin of the POV character, William Monk, experiencing what it was like to walk from one London environment to another. So let's see how the author, Anne Perry, approaches this change of scene.

> It was a beautiful day when he set out: a hot, high summer sun beating on the pavements, making the leafier squares pleasant refuges from the shimmering light hazy with the rising smoke of distant factory chimneys. Carriages clattered along the street past him, harnesses jingling, as people rode out to take the air or to pay early afternoon calls, drivers and footmen in livery, brasses gleaming. The smell of fresh horse droppings was pungent in the warmth

and a twelve-year-old crossing sweeper mopped his brow under
a floppy hat.
—Anne Perry, *A Sudden Fearful Death*

Now let's pull apart the details to determine how, in one paragraph, the
author places the reader into the Setting world of this historical novel.

It was a beautiful day [*This is what many writers might start with,
but it's generic and means little to the reader—what one person views
as beautiful may not be the same for another when they hear the
words "beautiful day."*] when he set out: a hot, high summer sun
[*Now she states it's hot, but again the author does not stop here.*]
beating [*Strong verb that shows how hot this day is.*] on the pave-
ments, making the leafier squares pleasant refuges [*The phrasing is
not expected from a contemporary man, but something one would
expect a well-educated male from the late 1800s to say.*] from the
shimmering light hazy with the rising smoke of distant factory
chimneys. [*A very specific detail that goes a step beyond the heat of
the day by expanding and letting the reader see, and possibly smell,
factory smoke, which paints a stronger image of industrial England.*]
Carriages clattered [*Strong auditory action verb.*] along the street
past him, harnesses jingling, [*The author did not stop with clattering
carriages, but added in the sounds of the horse harnesses to make
it very clear this is a world where people walking still rub shoulders
with carriages.*] as people rode out to take the air or to pay early
afternoon calls, [*Gives a reason for the carriage traffic that is a very
specific reference to a very specific time frame.*] drivers and footmen
in livery, brasses gleaming. [*And here she shows two more specific
visuals, not only an image of liveried servants but also their brasses,
a mark of a wealthier standard of living where the image of even
one's horses matters.*] The smell of fresh horse droppings was pungent [*Not the usual scent a contemporary stroller in today's London
would expect to inhale, but once pointed out, it's easy for the reader
to imagine the scent in the air.*] in the warmth and a twelve-year-old
crossing sweeper [*Child labor, another historical detail from this
time period of Charles Dickens and William Makepeace Thackeray.*]

mopped his brow under a floppy hat. [*The last final detail that brings home what was set up at the beginning of the paragraph, that the day was hot.*]

NOTE: The first time an important Setting—one important to your story—is described, a reader is willing to accept the story slowing down so that she can really see and experience that Setting. After a few paragraphs or a few pages, the reader will have already crafted her own images, so if the Setting matters, use sensory details in your descriptions sooner rather than later.

Here's a very different location, this time in New Orleans. This one is in a steampunk novel and the author not only enforces where the POV character is, but the sense of a different type of world.

> A faintly burning chemical stink joined the city's odors, trapped in the humid fog of Gulf water and river water that crept through the Quarter like a warm, wet bath.
> —Cherie Priest, *Ganymede*

Again, in this second example the reader is deep into the story, where an inexperienced writer might think the Setting has already been described, so that there is no need to use more words on it. But neither author missed the opportunity to thread in one or two quick and specific sentences to pull the reader into the story.

Utilizing Scents

Smell can convey a wealth of communication. Were you aware that after three months we retain only 30 percent of our visual memory, but even after a year we retain 100 percent of olfactory memory? Smell activates our primordial, or the oldest part of our brain, so if you are missing scents on the page, you're missing a very subtle but powerful element of sensory detail.

The following descriptions come from an interview with a Norwegian scent researcher. She is describing some of the locations she has visited to collect samples of scent.

> Havana. It smells sensual, of Cuba Libre [a rum, cola, and lime cocktail], coffee, dogs, and freshly washed laundry fluttering on endless balconies. The streets smell like they are crumbling, decaying, rotting. But unlike cities in the United States, Havana has been doing this for centuries. It rots in style. Berlin's Neukölln neighborhood is the closest you can get to Istanbul: sunflower oil, bread, dry cleaning, laundry detergent, tobacco, cheap aftershave, and kebabs. The outlying Colonia Hacienda de Echegaray district in Mexico City smells of fake leather boots, corn, dust, concrete, cocoa, burnt and moldy earth, plastic, sweat, chili peppers, and hot straw.

One or two sentences max and the reader is in Cuba, Istanbul, or Mexico City. When we smell *fake leather boots, burnt* or *moldy earth, plastic, sweat,* and *hot straw,* we add to those smells an image of run-down neighborhoods, stray dogs, a city that's a workingman's world. We fill in the blanks based on what we smell.

Scents can evoke memories so strongly. I love the smell of lilies, whereas my mother detests the same smell because they remind her of her mother's funeral. Have you ever been overwhelmed in a new location because everything is so new and different and the scents cause you to be overstimulated to the point you walk away with a pounding headache? Some scents mean pleasure to most people—baking cookies, the smell of a new book, the warm scent of babies' skin when you nuzzle their heads. Others evoke just the opposite response—the musty smell of damp basements, strong perfume in a small elevator, moldy bread.

Building a Believable Setting with Sensory Details

Sometimes you simply want to build a larger story Setting for the reader. This can happen when writing stories that readers tend to read for the Setting as much as the plot and characters. Examples include historical, steampunk, fantasy, science and some mystery series. Before we revisit Cherie Priest's steampunk novel set in New Orleans, let's imagine a rough-draft version:

> **FIRST DRAFT:** She walked through the French market and inhaled the smells she knew so well.

Not much here to let the reader experience a city during a time period where steam engines rule, viewed through the POV of a woman who's spent her whole life in this town and would never voluntarily leave it. So let's see how Priest uses specific sensory details for world building via Setting:

> The night smelled of gun oil and saddles, and the jasmine colognes of night ladies, or the violets and azaleas that hung from balconies in baskets; of berry liqueur and the verdant, herbal tang of absinthe delivered from crystal decanters, and the dried chilies hanging in the stalls of the French market, and powdered sugar and chicory.
> —Cherie Priest, *Ganymede*

Don't think that adding sensory detail means adding pages and pages of words. Do remember to be specific. *It smelled nice* or *of summer flowers* doesn't tell the reader much and the words are not working hard enough for your story.

> **NOTE:** Make sure that your sensory details are specific to the Setting of your story and filtered through a specific POV character's awareness.

Creating Backstory with Sensory Setting Details

In this next example we're in the mind, emotions, and skin of a young girl returning home after school—a pretty commonplace and ordinary event. In this case though, the author is building backstory by showing where this little girl came from, setting up a series of events in the future. What if the author had skipped over her opportunity and wrote something like:

> **FIRST DRAFT:** Polly returned from school but hesitated before going into her mom's trailer.

No emotion. No insights into this young girl's life. No reason to really care much about her.

> **SECOND DRAFT:** Polly's mom lived in a beaten-down trailer in a beaten-down trailer park.

Better. Now the reader understands the girl comes from a hard-scrabble background, but we're also being told, not shown. In some novels, where the backstory of the character is not as important to the current story, the previous example might be enough. Not every character needs a fully fleshed-out history, so be wary of using Setting to show characterization for every single character in your story.

> **NOTE:** The more words a writer allocates to a character or a situation, the more the reader understands to pay attention, because the details matter or will matter overall in the story.

So let's examine how Nevada Barr built in backstory for her protagonist, as well as created a character in this thriller that made the reader later wonder, *was this person a victim or a victimizer?*

Wind, cold for April, chased dirt and beer cans up the gravel street. Clutching her geometry book to her chest, Polly stood on the wooden step outside the door of her mother's trailer, her ear pressed against the aluminum. The icy bite of metal against her skin brought on a memory so sharp all she felt was its teeth.
—Nevada Barr, *13 ½*

Pull apart the sensory details.

Wind, cold for April, [*Tactile detail.*] chased dirt and beer cans up the gravel street. [*Visual and possibly auditory if you heard the sound of those cans whipping up the road.*] Clutching her geometry book to her chest, [*Tactile—can you feel the shape of that book and how she holds it?*] Polly stood on the wooden step outside the door of her mother's trailer, her ear pressed against the aluminum. The icy bite of metal against her skin brought on a memory so sharp all she felt was its teeth. [*More tactile detail that's all the more powerful for the fact that the reader was previously told that Polly was wearing a lightweight t-shirt.*]

Barr focused on multiple tactile sensory details to show a young girl, willing to experience piercing cold, yet unwilling to go inside her mother's trailer. Do you, as a reader, feel empathy for this girl? Are you in her skin feeling the wind, that book, the bite of cold metal? This is how a strong writer creates not only reader empathy for a character, but does so with active Setting.

Sounds in Setting

Next, watch how mystery writer Nancy Pickard quickly orients a reader to the Setting by focusing mostly on sounds.

Students looked up at us curiously from inside their classrooms as we walked past. Teachers' voices jarred the air, like different radio stations turned up too loud. Somewhere a couple of locker

A Writer's Guide to Active Setting

> doors slammed shut, and everywhere there was that smell that only
> schools have and that echoey sound and that odd slanting light in
> the halls.

—Nancy Pickard, *Confession*

Did you find yourself thinking about your own school environment and being tugged into the place quickly by the sensory details?

This is the power of adding sensory details to Setting description. Readers quickly find themselves pulled deeper into the Setting. They can feel themselves there on a three-dimensional level versus simply a visual level. If Pickard had chosen to remain only on a visual level, she might have written:

> Students looked up at us curiously from inside their classrooms as
> we walked past. There were lockers on both sides of the long hall
> and a scuffed linoleum floor. Overhead were fluorescent lights, most
> of them off in the middle of the day, but a few flickering.

Okay, but not great. As readers, we are seeing the Setting the way the POV character sees it, but we're not in the Setting the way sensory details can pull us in.

Let's turn to a different genre, urban fantasy, where the world contains both the expected and the unexpected, given that both humans and preternaturals exist in this story. This passage occurs several chapters into the story where, for some writers, it's easier to assume the reader already has a feel for the character and the location of the story events, so they slack off on making Setting work hard. Not this *New York Times* best-selling author. Watch how in one paragraph the reader is quickly re-anchored into the story Setting, taking place in contemporary Seattle.

> Above my head I heard whispers, and the rasp of claws against
> stone; and another kind of hum in the air that was partially from
> the throats of demons in my hair, but mostly the city: engines rum-
> bling low and warm, and the energy running through the veins of
> the buildings around whose roots we walked. I heard laughter, glass

breaking, a throb of music from the open door of a bar; a groan
from an alley and the long liquid rush of urine hitting concrete; and
a small dog, barking furiously from an apartment above our heads.
—Marjorie M. Liu, *Armor of Roses*

See how many sensory details the author uses to make sure the reader
knows the character is in a seedy part of big city? She doesn't stop there,
though, making sure the reader really hears what kinds of engines—
rumbling low and warm. The reader doesn't need to know if these are
trucks or muscle cars, what they do need to know is that specific sound is
in this Setting. The author keeps going—*thrum of hot electricity, laughter,
glass breaking, a throb of music from* a specific kind of location, *a groan
from an alley,* the sound of someone urinating, *and a small dog, barking.*

What if the author skipped all these rich, sensory details and wrote
the following instead?

> **ROUGH DRAFT:** I could hear the city as I walked past buildings,
> a bar, an alley, and an apartment above my head.

Can you see how hard the sensory details work to pull you deeper into
the story? How much is lost by ignoring the power of Setting and sensory detail?

> **NOTE:** Active Setting forces a writer to develop deeper POV, which
> creates a stronger bond between the characters and the reader.

Putting the Sensory Setting Details Together

Now let's look at how T. Jefferson Parker uses sensory details to describe
the scene of a crime from the POV of a police investigator:

> She noted that the table had been set for two. A pair of seductive
> high heels stood near the couch, facing her, like a ghost was stand-
> ing in them, watching. The apartment was still, the slider closed
> against the cool December night. Good for scent. She closed her
> eyes. Salt air. Baked fowl. Coffee. Goddamned rubber gloves, of

course. A whiff of gunpowder? Maybe a trace of perfume, or the flowers on the table—gardenia, rose, lavender? And of course, the obscenity of spilled blood—intimate, meaty, shameful.

She listened to the waves. To the traffic. To the little kitchen TV turned low; an evangelist bleating for money. To the clunk of someone in the old walkway. To her heart, fast and heavy in her chest. Merci felt most alive when working for the dead. She'd always loved an underdog.

—T. Jefferson Parker, *Red Light*

The above description does not stop the reader, but orients them deeply into the *where*, *who*, and *what* of the crime and the characters in one powerful paragraph. Parker doesn't just describe the apartment space clinically, but layers in strong sensory details. The effect pulls the reader more deeply into the scene. The reader is standing there with the detective: hearing what she's hearing, smelling what she's smelling, feeling the texture of the gloves on her hands. The reading experience has changed from simply looking at the Setting to being in the Setting.

Here's another great example:

The come-and-get-it smell of espresso welcomed her. Fall Out Boy was playing on the stereo, "Hum Hallelujah." Lieutenant Amy Tang stood at the counter, fingers double tapping, waiting for her order.

—Meg Gardiner, *The Memory Collector*

How many sensory details did Gardiner manage to slide into the reader's awareness in three very short sentences? What is amazing is that the author could have painted a visual picture alone:

ROUGH DRAFT: She entered the coffee shop, which looked and smelled like a million other coffee shops, and saw the Lieutenant waiting for her.

But Gardiner went deeper with her writing and placed the reader in the scene, not with an overload of visual prompts, but with a smell and two sound prompts. What Gardiner managed in the three sentences above was to anchor the reader into the new space through the senses. We all know the smell of a coffee shop, and by reminding the reader of that specific scent, she "smells" that place, instantly transporting herself there.

What about the sound prompt? What does that do? Is it okay that the reader doesn't know the band? Can you still get a sense of Setting by the POV character's reaction to the music playing? What if you change the band's name to something else—Sex Pistols or Coldplay? Or Chuck Mangione or Frank Sinatra? Just by changing what the reader mentally "hears" in this coffee shop you change the experience of it.

> **NOTE:** There's power in the use of three beats in writing. A sound and two smells. A texture and two sounds. Don't over use it, but when you want to make a quick, clear anchor for the reader, the three-beat style can be powerful.

Here's another example of sensory detail. Tess Gerritsen writes bullet-paced thrillers that rarely showcase a whole paragraph of detail, so when she does the reader pays attention, knowing that this Setting matters:

> The school bell clanged, calling the students in from recess. He stood calming himself, inhaling deeply. He focused on the fragrance of fresh-cut hay, of bread baking in the nearby communal kitchen. From across the compound, where the new workshop hall was being built, came the whine of a saw and the echoes of a dozen hammers pounding nails. The virtuous sounds of honest labor, of a community working toward His greater glory.
>
> —Tess Gerritsen, *Ice Cold*

In the above example the reader can smell, hear, see, and almost taste the growing community, but the Setting description does more. It places the reader into a scene that might not be familiar to him, since he has not personally lived in such an environment, but the different sounds are very familiar and have strong connotations. A school-bell's ring, the scent of baking bread, hammers and saws at work—all are sounds that are industrious, pleasant, and denote a certain amount of comfort. This environment might sound idyllic, but to the individuals living there, it proves anything but as the story unfolds. From ideal to hellish, the reader will remember what this place sounds like and contrast it to what's revealed later in the story.

Layering POV and Sensory Details

Auditory sensory details can enhance a story in so many ways. We focused on how to use Setting description to reveal character earlier, but we also need to ensure that we're accurately describing the sensory details through a very particular set of eyes. Think of New York City's Times Square, or the heart of any other large city that is alive with sounds. The awareness of those sounds will change depending on where the POV character is coming from, what they are doing, and how they feel.

After a long frustrating day, standing in Times Square can be like nails scratching down a chalkboard on your nerves. But if you've landed a dream job in a city you feel is your city, the sounds of this tiny speck of space can be seductive and empowering. On the other hand, what would you hear if your young child has just wandered off? Or if you were looking for a runaway teenager last seen hawking himself in Times Square? What might you hear in these few blocks?

The place hasn't changed at all, and neither have the sounds. What has changed is how the author relates those sounds to the reader and threads them through her descriptive details. If you change a character's POV you should change the sensory details to pull and anchor the reader in the character and the story.

Here is a small snippet from a debut story that has been described as mesmerizing and evocative. One of the reasons is the use of sensory details. This passage takes place in 1942 in Seattle, right after a Chinese boy's first date with a young Japanese girl. The POV character loves jazz and that love is something he shares with his home city of Seattle, the time frame of the story, and his new Japanese friend. It also creates a distance between himself and his very traditional father. Watch how the author uses those facts to weave meaning into the sensory details here.

First we're going to start with a hypothetical rough draft:

FIRST DRAFT: Henry left his bedroom and walked down the alley.

What do you think? Do you know where you are? Any sense of the city surrounding him?

SECOND DRAFT: Henry left his bedroom and walked down the dark alley near where he'd been in the Jazz club earlier.

Better but still pretty blasé. If you were reading the book, you'd mentally orient Henry to where he'd been earlier on the evening, but not much else. You're not in his skin walking down this alley. So let's examine how Jamie Ford lets the reader experience what his protagonist is experiencing.

Henry left his bedroom window up, feeling the cool air come off the water. He could smell the rain that would be coming soon and hear the horns and bells of the ferries along the waterfront signaling their last run for the night. And in the distance he could hear swing jazz being played somewhere, maybe even the Black Elks Club.
—Jamie Ford, *Hotel on the Corner of Bitter and Sweet*

Are you in Henry's skin now? The example above was a nice scene ending that creates part of the evocative feel to this book. Let's look closer at how this is achieved:

Henry left his bedroom window up, feeling the cool air come off the water. [*Anyone who lives or has visited an ocean-side locale can really feel the temperature drop in the evening. Here Henry is in an apartment building in Chinatown, only a few blocks from the shores of Seattle's Elliott Bay so this small sensory detail adds a lot.*] He could smell the rain that would be coming soon and hear the horns and bells of the ferries along the waterfront signaling their last run for the night. [*Again a very specific Seattle sound, and one that places this story in that city, versus a different ocean-side locale.*] And in the distance he could hear swing jazz being played somewhere, maybe even the Black Elks Club. [*This location is where he had been with his friend. The memory of a sound here layers a lot in the story and ends the scene on a very sensory detail.*]

Here's another example where the ordinary becomes extraordinary in bringing the reader deeper into the story.

ROUGH DRAFT: More sheriffs' vehicles drove into view.

The reader is being told, not shown. This can be a shorthand description if you want the focus on a different element of the story. But if you want the reader to experience the story as the POV character is, look how, by adding sound, author Patricia McLinn brings the Setting to life.

> The throaty drone of more vehicular beasts coming up the road announced a sheriff's department four-wheel drive.
> —Patricia McLinn, *Sign Off*

Most readers at one time or another have found themselves waiting to hear the arrival of another vehicle, regardless of the situation. But in the above example, McLinn takes the situation, with news reporters waiting for information at a crime scene, and ratchets up the tension of what could be a nonevent by adding in sensory detail.

Watch how Nevada Barr uses contrasting sensory details to show the reader where the POV character Anna is now, and also to vividly underline the difference between where she has lived in the past and its effect on her:

> Closing the door quietly behind her, Anna paused a minute to breathe in New Orleans in spring after the rain. In the mountains and deserts of the West there would be the ozone and pine, sage and dust—scents that cleared her head and the vision made the heart race and the horizon impossibly far away and alluring.

Here spring's perfume was lazy and narcotic, hinting of hidden things, languid hours, and secrets whispered on breath smelling of bourbon and mint. In Rocky Mountain National Park, the clean dry air scoured the skin, polished bone, and honed Anna's senses to a keen edge. Here it caressed nurturing flesh with moisture, curling wind-sere hair. It coddled and swathed till believing in dreams and magic seemed inevitable.

—Nevada Barr, *Burn*

If the author in the last excerpt had simply chosen to describe the scents of New Orleans, this would have been good sensory detail. But by using the sensory details in contrast to where she had been before, and obviously loved, to where she was now, the reader receives so much more. There is a stronger sense of characterization and an awareness of being someplace mysterious, sensual, and possibly a little dangerous. In Texas and New Mexico, where Anna has lived and worked in earlier books in this mystery series, she is very much in her comfort zone. In this new Setting in New Orleans, the extra-sensory overload is making her dreamier, less sure of herself. The author has shown the reader that the POV character is feeling out of her depth through Setting description.

Here's another example of sensory detail adding to the page. In this paragraph, three characters have escaped from a French prison in a historical romance. The POV character is a French woman; the other characters are English spies, enemies of the French woman. Notice how the author threads in sensory detail, as well as foreshadowing complications in a paragraph that's mostly Setting. This passage is the POV of one of the English spies, who starts the dialogue.

Her night vision was extraordinary. "I can't see a thing."

"Stop trying to see, English. Listen instead. The night is telling stories all around you. The Rue Berenger lies ahead. ... Oh ... fifty paces perhaps. The baker on the corner is even now baking bread. One can smell that. Rue Berenger runs east to the bridge, to Paris, where men in your profession likely have friends. Or you go uphill

to the west, and you will come after a time to England, where you have even more friends, beyond doubt.
—Joanna Bourne, *The Spymaster's Lady*

Now what if Bourne decided to use only a visual Setting? The prose would be as dry as someone reciting directions—*go straight ahead until you reach the bridge and keep going till you reach Paris.* Ho hum. No scent of bread wafting on the early-morning air.

Taste is not often the first sensory detail one latches onto when writing Setting, but it can be powerful nonetheless. Think of taste like a fine herb used judiciously by a master chef—a little can go a long way.

Let's see how James Lee Burke uses taste, or the reader's memory of taste, along with other sensory descriptions to pull the reader deep into the Setting of New Orleans. But before we jump to his words, and the reason he's known for the locations of his stories, let's look at an imaginary rough draft.

> **ROUGH DRAFT:** At an outdoor table in the Café du Monde I watched morning give way to day. It was a picturesque street.

So what do you think? Are you in New Orleans in this terse example? Or are you shuddering, as no doubt Burke would be, at how dry and blah the passage is?

Let's see how Burke pulls us into his character's POV and the city in the example below:

> At an outdoor table in the Café du Monde, over beignets and coffee with hot milk, I would watch the pinkness of the morning spread across the Quarter, the unicyclists pirouetting in front of the cathedral, jugglers tossing wood balls in the air, street bands who played for tips knocking out "Tin Roof Blues" and "Rampart Street Parade." The balconies along the streets groaned with the weight of potted plants, and bougainvillea hung in huge clumps from the iron grillwork and bloomed as brightly as drops of blood in the sunlight. Corner grocery stores, run by Italian families, still had wood-bladed

fans on the ceilings and sold boudin and po'boy sandwiches to working people. Out front, in the shade of the colonnade, were bins of cantaloupe, bananas, strawberries and rattlesnake watermelons.

—James Lee Burke, *Pegasus Descending*

Breaking the example up, let's examine how the author weaves a very clear, detailed place by threading in a lot of sight detail, but also some sound, scent, and possible taste detail, too.

At an outdoor table in the Café du Monde, [*The reader is anchored by a very specific Setting location here.*] over beignets and coffee with hot milk, [*This sensory detail can be either scent or taste or both, depending on whether a reader has tasted beignets or coffee with hot milk.*] I would watch the pinkness of the morning spread across the Quarter, the unicyclists pirouetting in front of the cathedral, [*Two visual details.*] jugglers tossing wood balls in the air, street bands who played for tips knocking out "Tin Roof Blues" and "Rampart Street Parade." [*If a reader has ever heard the whir and thud associated with juggling wood balls, this starts two sound details. Otherwise, there's one more sight and a sound of the band.*] The balconies along the streets groaned with the weight of potted plants, and bougainvillea hung in huge clumps from the iron grillwork and bloomed as brightly as drops of blood in the sunlight. [*More visual details.*] Corner grocery stores, run by Italian families, still had wood-bladed fans on the ceilings and sold boudin and po'boy sandwiches to working people. [*And again, this detail can be sight only, or sight with taste (or smell), for those familiar with this type of deli.*] Out front, in the shade of the colonnade, were bins of cantaloupe, bananas, strawberries and rattlesnake watermelons.

Not every story needs as much or as evocative a Setting description to allow the reader to be in the skin of the POV character. Because Burke's protagonist knows this city well, and has lived in Louisiana, the reader believes in the character because of how the author describes a city.

Let's look at another example, one in a novel with a shorter word count than Burke's, from the POV of a character who knows the Setting, which will play only a small part in the external plot line.

> **NOTE:** Always keep in mind how much particular Setting your story needs. Don't know how much? Read published authors who are writing types of stories similar to your own and study how much Setting they use. It's an approximation, but it can be very helpful.

In this next example from one of my novels, we're looking at sensory detail involving a tactile description implying taste, among other senses, that's set deep into the novel and used to quickly orient the reader to a new location. Here, taste is a tactile scent implied by the quality of the air, and what's in the air that can be tasted on the tongue.

> India—bleating animals wandering the streets, car horns blaring, dust mingling with masses of people, wrapping one in a blanket both suffocating and irritating. The monsoons had not yet broken the dry heat; an air of expectancy choked human and animal alike.
>
> —Mary Buckham, *Invisible Recruit*

The intention of this Setting description was to let the readers know the characters have arrived in India, but I did not want to spend a lot of page space describing things, buildings, or images. The intention was to anchor the reader in the fact that the characters were now in a totally alien (to them) environment and to set the emotional feel of that change. How many sensory details did I use? Can you pick out sound? Taste? (Dust.) Feel? (Blanket of dust and dry heat.) Smells? (Animals and dust again.) Two sentences and then back to the action of the story, but the reader is now in India instead of simply seeing India.

When you think of the sense of touch in a Setting, think of one's whole body and not just the fingers or the hand. Don't tell the reader that it's ninety degrees in the shade if you can show characters fanning themselves and blotting perspiration from their faces. If your character has grown up in dry heat, have their whole body gob-smacked with the change when they first travel to a location dripping with humidity. Standing on an ocean beach you could feel warm, moisture-laden breezes, or salt-tainted blasts of frigid, damp air—two very different beaches shown simply by touch and feel.

Instead of telling the reader your character is exhausted and crawling into bed, can you show his emotional state by what he feels? There's a world of difference between finally creeping under the security of a well-loved eiderdown comforter on a cold night as opposed to falling into a creaking bed and yanking a scratchy, flimsy, paper-thin blanket over his shoulders that then exposes his toes to the freezing air.

Don't worry about sensory details in your first draft as you're juggling choreography, characterization, and so much more, but definitely think sensory in your revision process.

Ways to Bring Out Sensory Details

Think in terms of which sensory details a POV character would notice in the particular Setting at that particular time.

> **NOTE:** The smallest sensory detail can evoke a change in the emotional state of a character. We all know this instinctively, but using this simple technique can reap big rewards by deepening the reader's understanding for and empathy with the POV character.

- If you change the time and emotional state of the POV character, you should see a difference in which sensory details are being noticed.

- Use the sensory details when you first change a location, open a chapter, or to indicate a shift in the emotional state of the POV character. An example might be listening to specific music at the opening of the scene. A scene that ends lonely and low-energy can begin soft and relaxing.

A Writer's Guide to Active Setting

Texture is so very often overlooked in Setting but can act as a metaphor or quickly orient a reader to the time of day, a change in location, or reveal more information about the POV character.

The bottom line is that sensory detail can enhance your Setting descriptions and thus the readers' experience of your story in so many ways.

What Not to Do

Avoid using too little sensory detail so the reader is held at arm's length, waiting for clarification.

> The room stunk and I was getting hot.

The next example has more words, but the words might pull the reader too deep into the scene.

> The room stunk, smelling of day-old cabbage and weak tea, while the radiator chugged out enough heat to make the room feel like Atlanta in the summer.

Below, the writer is bringing in sensory details but it's via a formulaic approach that also creates a pronoun-verb, sensory-detail sentence pattern that the reader quickly notices. Remember to change up your sensory details and how you reveal them to the reader.

> **OPENING OF CHAPTER TWO:** He smelled the dead fish.
> **OPENING OF CHAPTER FOUR:** He smelled the fresh laundry.
> **OPENING OF CHAPTER NINETEEN:** She smelled stale socks.

Assignment

Part 1

Place yourself in either a familiar Setting or a new one, but someplace you feel comfortable closing your eyes. Now see if you can describe the following:

- Sound
- Touch/Texture
- Smells
- Taste

Be specific and don't stop with just one answer—go deeper. Example: a grocery store parking lot. First sound is cars driving past or parking. Going deeper: the rattle of grocery carts, birds crying overhead, the squeal of a child released from a car, or the squawk when they're put into a car against their wishes. Tires driving over gravel-sprinkled parking lots in a wintery climate sound different than tires swishing through puddles in a rainy lot.

Now use the same Setting and put one of your characters in that Setting. What would they see, hear, feel, smell, or taste based on their POV?

OR: Have a friend or family member do this exercise with you. Both of you in the same location, taking notes and then comparing. The one with the most details wins!

Part 2

Use any two to four sentences of Setting currently in your WIP—one without much sensory detail and preferably one at the opening of a scene, chapter, or change of location for the character.

See what sensory details you can create without adding a lot more words. [**NOTE:** This may require rewriting and replacing some visual details with other sensory details.] Put yourself in the POV character's state of mind and look around. What would he specifically smell, touch, hear, or taste? Write an example of each sense, then add to your current scene. Try for a minimum of two additional details, or more if you wish.

Do you like the rewrite? Did you discover it added more depth to the story or insights into your character?

INTENTION: To show the power of using sensory details while keeping you aware that if you change the character, you'll change which senses she uses or how she relates to the sensory details of a specific Setting.

Recap

- Thread specific sounds through descriptive details that can pull and anchor the reader onto the page.
- As you change your Setting, look for opportunities where you can quickly orient and anchor the reader to where the characters are by focusing on sensory details of each specific Setting.
- Change up your sensory details so you are not always using the same senses.
- By using more sensory details in your Setting description, readers will feel themselves pulled deeper into a story on a three-dimensional level versus simply a visual level.
- Make sure that your detail is specific to the place and specific to the POV character's awareness.

EMOTION, CONFLICT, & BACKSTORY

Overview

In strong writing there is always an overlap of craft techniques, and therefore more integration of the whole. Nothing lives in isolation. This is necessary both for combining the elements into a seamless unit and for helping you assimilate by repetition.

We're looking at very different examples in this next section, so you don't need to have read the earlier excerpts to understand and embrace the concepts here, but these concepts build on one another. They are blocks used to create a strong structure. The more you learn about writing Active Setting, the more you will be able to add depth and texture to your writing as you explore opportunities to use the material.

04

Using Setting to Show Emotion

Using Setting to show emotion is one of the most powerful tools of Active Setting, although it is underused by many writers.

Most readers consciously or subconsciously read for the emotion of your story. They look at the cover to clue them into whether a story is humorous, light, dark, or edgy. Within a story though, emotions can run the gamut from light (happy, relief, joy) to dark (anger, fear, terror) as you lead your characters, and thus the reader, on your story journey. There's enormous energy created on the page through the conscious choice of words to ratchet up the emotions you want the reader to experience, all while the characters move through the story.

Creating an Emotional Experience

Let's jump right in and explore how some amazing authors, writing in a variety of genres, use Setting to show emotion.

> Outside, the wind was howling and another line of black clouds was trooping over the city. Big slabs of bruise-colored clouds.
> —Jeffery Deaver, *The Coffin Dancer*

In the above example, Deaver, a suspense/thriller writer, uses weather to clue the reader into the tone of the story by foreshadowing. Things are not only bad, but are looking as if they are going to get worse. Weather in Setting, along with specific descriptive word choices, is one of the easiest ways to orient the reader to the mood of a scene.

What would have happened if Deaver had not been as meticulous in his word choices?

> Outside, the wind blew, and another line of clouds was moving over the city. Big clouds.

Any emotion? No. We see clouds, but that image does not enhance the emotion of the story in any way. Look to the descriptive words being used, as many writers depend only on their adjectives. Instead of relying solely on adjectives, consider powering up your verb choices to get more emotion into a Setting description. *Clouds hunkering over the horizon* is a stronger image than *big clouds on the horizon* or *fluffy clouds on the horizon.*

> **NOTE:** Settings, used well, help pull out the emotions you want the reader to experience.

Let's see another example, envisioning a rough-draft version first. The POV character is driving to the home of a young boy who has run away.

> **ROUGH DRAFT:** It was a gray-clapboard apartment building in a bad location. It faced north and must have been cold when winter came. Today was very warm.

Any emotion here? We get a concrete image of the building but that's about all. So let's see how Nancy Pickard not only shows the building, but creates emotional tension on the page.

> It was big, three stories of dingy old gray clapboard set like a rotten tooth in a nearly empty mouth: This was a decimated block, with empty buildings and blowing litter. It faced north and must have been cold as a sailor's nose on an icy winter's night. On this day, with the temperatures in the upper nineties, we heard the laboring of air conditioners in the windows.
> —Nancy Pickard, *Confession*

Let's dig deeper into the above example to see how the author maximized Setting to make it work harder:

> It was big, three stories of dingy old gray clapboard [*Here Pickard doesn't stop at one adjective, but beats home the points she wants to make—dingy, old, gray—before she gives the specific type of building.*] set like a rotten tooth in a nearly empty mouth: [*Here she drills home how the POV character feels about what she's seeing. There's no doubt this impacts how she's thinking about the runaway boy and what she will do for him.*] This was a decimated [*Specific adjective choice.*] block, with empty buildings and blowing litter. [*Note the double beat here—empty and blowing. If she'd eased off and had written buildings and litter the emotion would be toned down.*] It faced north and must have been cold as a sailor's nose on an icy winter's night. [*Again, an internal thought from a specific POV that hammers home how she feels about the place.*] On this day, with the temperatures in the upper nineties, we heard the laboring [*Strong action verb.*] of air conditioners in the windows.

Succinct Emotion

Before you assume that emotion in Setting needs sentence upon sentence, or whole paragraphs to reveal the emotion or subtext of a story, let's look at how *New York Times* best-selling author Marjorie M. Liu shows emotions through specific details in a short, concise sentence. It's important to remember that if you've already established a Setting—a specific location—there's no need to extensively redescribe detail when a character returns to that location. If you look back at the Liu example used in the last chapter on sensory details, you'll see that the first experience for the reader into this area of Seattle warranted more words, details, and page space. And all of it was created with showing. This means that here, as the protagonist travels through a familiar Setting, the author can sit back and do more telling than showing.

From the Liu example in the last chapter, the reader has a strong sense of this location, so the author chooses to use specific words to describe where the character was. Then she moves on with the story.

> I was still in the warehouse district, a crumbling neighborhood of
> pale concrete, shattered sidewalks, and broken windows.
> —Marjorie M. Liu, *The Iron Hunt*

Look at Liu's word choices—*crumbling, pale concrete, shattered, broken.* What if she used very different words, like this?

> I was still in the warehouse district, a high-end neighborhood of
> artsy concrete slabs, brick sidewalks, and view-hogging windows.

OR:

> I was still in the warehouse district, a vibrant neighborhood of
> thriving industrial concrete buildings, crowded sidewalks, and
> sparkling windows.

Do you get a very different sense of the emotion of the POV character by what she focuses on? Is there a difference in the feeling, or emotion, of the Setting between the three different examples? In Liu's original description, do you expect good things to happen for the character around the next corner? If the character is looking for a rental unit, what would it say about her if she chooses the first neighborhood, rather than the second?

> **NOTE:** Telling and showing, or telling after something has been shown, can work in a novel.

Theme and Mood

Let's look at another example of Setting, with and without emotion.

> … I stood staring out the sliding glass doors. The backyard looked
> melancholy in the late autumn, the foliage thinned out and the

high fence depressingly obvious. The gray pool cover was spotted with puddles of rainwater. The warm colors of the big room were more pleasant, and I roamed around it picking up odds and ends as I stretched chilled muscles.

—Charlaine Harris, *Shakespeare's Champion*

In the above example, the initial mood shown by examining the Setting outside the sliding-glass doors reflects the emotional tenor of the POV character in this scene. Pensive. Melancholy. A little down. Later in this passage the author changes the tone by having the character become more active. Warm. Pleasant. Because of these few sentences, the reader is prepped for some change in the story, since the tone moves from low-key and somber to the feeling of safety within the room. This mirrors what is being set up in the story, because within a page, danger will approach the house from outside—an outside Setting the reader is already aware of and already knows is dark.

What would have happened if Harris had written it this way?

ROUGH DRAFT: I stood looking out the sliding-glass doors at the backyard. The autumn trees looked bare, showing the fence in back. The pool cover was covered with water. The warm colors of the big room were more pleasant, and I roamed around it picking up odds and ends as I stretched chilled muscles.

See? The reader gets a visual of the backyard but no sense of emotion. There's no contrast between what's happening outside and where the character is inside.

Setting can do so much to emotionally set the mood or theme of a story, which in turn makes it easier for the reader to accept what is unfolding or about to unfold. Have you ever read a story, or a scene in a story, that's meant to be suspenseful, frightening, or relaxing, but the only information you received was a bald comment on the POV character's emotions? Or worse: no cues at all to the emotional tenor of the story? Most published stories avoid this, but many inexperienced writers assume that telling the reader the character is scared or relaxed is enough. It's not.

The next sentence paints a very specific sense of the mood or emotion of a Setting based on word choices. Given that the story takes place in Cambodia, note how the author intentionally reveals, in a fresh way, one small detail about the type of day it is.

> Today the water hung in the air like torn strips of gray paper.
> —Colin Cotterill, *Love Song from A Shallow Grave*

What are the emotions that come to mind with this simple but poignant description? Melancholy? Subdued? Despondent? What if the author chose to use a less evocative way to describe the weather?

FIRST DRAFT: Today was gray.

Are you in the Setting? Do you get a strong sense of the emotional tone the POV character feels? Probably not.

SECOND DRAFT: The day was rainy and gray.

This is where some writers might stop, leaving the reader to transfer their own emotions to the Setting. And sometimes that's exactly what you need to do. But not every time. If the POV character acts based on her perception of the emotion of the Setting, then it's invaluable to spend a little more time, even just a few more words, to make that clear to the reader. One of the ways to do this is based on the character's perception of his Setting.

NOTE: Emotions drive actions in a story. Don't forget to use your Setting details to show those emotions.

Using Concrete Descriptions

Let's see how mystery author M.C. Beaton uses just a few sentences to bring the reader into the Setting and to show the emotional mood of the POV character. But before we see how Beaton shows this, let's look at a possible first draft.

FIRST DRAFT: The day was depressing. The city of Strathbane was also depressing and looked ugly, too.

Not much here. No visuals and the reader has been told, but not shown, the city and the POV character's response to the city. So let's revisit:

SECOND DRAFT: He became more depressed the closer he drove to Strathbane, a mid-sized city with high unemployment and over-run with drug users.

Better, but the reader is not fully drawn into what the POV character is seeing. So now let's look closely at how M.C. Beaton draws the readers emotionally into the mood she wants them to feel, as she shows what her protagonist is feeling via his view of the Setting.

> The day suited his mood. The brief spell of good weather had changed to a damp drizzle. Wraiths of mist crawled down the flanks of the mountain.
> Strathbane had once been a busy fishing port, but new European fishing quotas had destroyed businesses. Then under a scheme to regenerate the Highlands, new businesses were set up, but drugs had arrived before them and the town became a depressed area of rotting factories, vandalized high-rises, and dangerous, violent youth.
> —M.C. Beaton, *Death of a Maid*

Anyone who follows this mystery series featuring Scottish Highlands constable Hamish Macbeth knows that he will do anything to avoid being promoted and sent to work in the nearby large city of Strathbane. But even someone new to the series gets a strong emotional sense of what the city looks like, and how he feels about it, by how he sees the town. Let's analyze this passage further.

The day suited his mood. [*This sets up the reader to clearly understand that an emotional explanation is coming, but instead of simply telling and ending the Setting description here, the author then uses showing.*] The brief spell of good weather had changed to a damp drizzle. [*The use of contrast not only indicates a change in the story, but the passage of time.*] Wraiths [*Strong image here that holds a negative connotation.*] of mist crawled [*Powerful verb.*] down the flanks of the mountain.

Strathbane had once been a busy fishing port, but new European fishing quotas had destroyed businesses. [*Backstory specific to this recurring Setting.*] Then under a scheme to regenerate the Highlands, new businesses were set up, but drugs had arrived before them and the town became a depressed [*Specific adjective.*] area of rotting [*Specific adjective.*] factories, vandalized [*Specific adjective.*] high-rises, and dangerous, violent [*Specific adjectives.*] youth.

Look what happens if we remove the adjectives used in just the last sentence: *the town became an area of factories, high-rises, and youth.*

There's nothing dark or depressing in this description, which means readers might get a vague visual image of a city, but without more details they are left to create their own visuals. Kansas City, New Orleans, London, and Hong Kong are all cities that have factories, high-rises, and youth, but they are radically different cities. You'll want to go even deeper here for the strongest description on the page. There's a world of difference between empty, barren factories or sleek, state-of-the-art factories churning out electronic goods. By taking only one concrete image, a factory, and changing the specific words used to describe it, the reader is more deeply invested in the world inhabited by the character. A large chunk of that investment is based on the emotional feel of what she is seeing.

> **NOTE:** Avoid the mistake of describing only the things the character sees. Take the next small step and add the POV character's emotional meaning to those things.

Backstory as Memory and Setting

Let's see how Walter Mosley uses a POV character's memory of an event involving Setting to give the reader a strong sense of the current Setting, as well as the emotion of the current events. He also layers in a hint of backstory, which we'll discuss in more depth later.

> Psychedelic posters for concerts were plastered to walls. Here and there brave knots of tourists walked through, marveling at the counterculture they'd discovered.
>
> I was reminded of a day when a mortar shell in the ammunition hut of our base camp in northern Italy exploded for no apparent reason. No one was killed but a shock ran through the whole company. All of a sudden whatever we had been doing or thinking, wherever we had been going was forgotten. One man started laughing uncontrollably, another went to the mess tent and wrote a letter to his mother. I kept noticing things I'd never seen before. For instance, the hand-painted sign above the infirmary read HOS-PItAL, all in capital letters except for the t. That one character was in lower case. I had seen that sign a thousand times but only after the explosion did I really look at it.
>
> The Haight was another kind of explosion, a stunning surge of intuition that broke down all the ways you thought life had to be.
> —Walter Mosley, *Cinnamon Kiss*

Mosley is using Setting here in so many powerful ways. Instead of writing a traditional description of what the POV character is currently seeing, Mosley starts with a very specific detail—posters. And not any kind of posters, but psychedelic ones. He then segues into a description of a Setting in the past, one that appears to have nothing to do with the present. He does this to evoke a response in the reader. Most readers can remember an emotionally powerful experience where, after the experience, they zeroed in on a detail. Then, that detail became the metaphor for how they thought about life before and how their perceptions changed. The reader has no doubt after this flashback that the character feels strongly about the Haight-Ashbury district and that the "brave tourists," the ones who don't belong there, just as he feels he doesn't, also have a strong emotional reaction.

NOTE: Consider using emotional Setting in your backstory passages to enhance or contrast them with your current story Setting, or to create an emotional echo as Mosley has done.

Utilizing Specific Details

Here's another author, thriller writer Harlan Coben, who focuses readers on a specific Setting detail and then expands the emotional note of that detail.

> In fact, the door was beyond ordinary, wood and four-paneled, the kind of door you see standing guard in front of three out of every four suburban homes, with faded paint and a knocker at chest level no one ever used and a faux brass knob. But as I walked toward it, a distant streetlight barely illuminated my way, that dark opening yawning like a mouth ready to gobble me whole, the feeling of doom was unshakeable. Each step forward took great effort, as if I were walking not along a somewhat crackled walk but through wet-cement.
>
> —Harlan Coben, *Caught*

Coben writes about everyman characters caught in complex traps where each step forward is fraught with greater and greater risk and loss, but there's no way back either. Let's look at what he does so well.

> In fact, the door was beyond ordinary, [*He starts with telling the reader. This situation could happen to anyone.*] wood and four-paneled, [*Here he shows what he's talking about, luring the reader into a stronger image and feel that they have seen this kind of door, too.*] the kind of door you see standing guard in front of three out of every four suburban homes, [*Here the POV character's internalization reinforces that he should be feeling one thing based on what he's*

seeing.] with faded paint and a knocker at chest level no one ever used and a faux brass knob. [*And here Coben hammers home the small, ordinary details that should not be frightening. But notice how he changes the emotional note in the next sentence.*] But as I walked toward it, a distant [*Specific word choice indicating how isolated he feels.*] streetlight barely illuminated [*Expanding the emotion of loneliness.*] my way, that dark [*Specific word choice contrasting with what has already been seen.*] opening yawning like a mouth ready to gobble me whole, [*And right here the internalization spins the emotional feel from ordinary to something very different.*] the feeling of doom was unshakeable. [*Drives home the emotion here.*] Each step forward took great effort, [*Telling that builds on the emotion.*] as if I were walking not along a somewhat crackled walk but through wet-cement. [*Ending on an emotional note diametrically opposed to the ordinary Setting details established at the beginning of this paragraph.*]

Here's another emotionally charged passage where Setting reveals the emotion churning through the POV character. But before we get to how Jonathan Tropper describes his late father's sporting-goods store, let's write a generic description of the store.

> **FIRST DRAFT:** The shop had awnings that were clean. In the windows was a display of winter sporting gear. Elmsbrook was a picturesque town.

The best that can be said of the above is that it's short. The reader will not walk away with a strong sense of a specific town or the emotional meaning behind what the POV character sees.

> **SECOND DRAFT:** The hunter-green awnings of the shop have recently been cleaned, and the windows are crammed with winter sports gear. Elmsbrook is the perfect town. It's always picturesque with clean sidewalks and clock towers.

Better. Now the reader gets a stronger feel for a lovely town where everything sounds nice, based on the word choices: *cleaned, clean, perfect,
picturesque*. But that's not the emotional image Jonathan Tropper was
going for when he wrote the passage below:

> The hunter-green awnings of the shop, usually speckled with dried
> bird droppings and water stains, have recently been cleaned, and
> the windows, anticipating the fall season, are crammed with hockey,
> ski and snowboard gear. The mannequin in the corner is wearing a
> goalie mask, and in the ominous flicker of the fluorescent light he
> looks like Jason, the serial killer from those Friday the 13th movies.
> Elmsbrook is the perfect town for a serial killer, and I mean that
> in the best possible way. It's always the picturesque towns, with
> clean sidewalks and clock towers, where Jason and Freddy come
> to slaughter oversexed teenagers.
> —Jonathan Tropper, *This Is Where I Leave You*

The above passage is not from a mystery or a thriller, but in a funny,
heart-wrenching coming-of-age drama about a middle-aged man. By
contrasting how idyllic and picture-perfect his town looks with a reference to a slasher movie, the first-person POV character reveals how
he feels about the town and revisiting the place he most associates with
his estranged father, who has recently died. Tropper's work is often described as dark literary humor. Can you see how the Setting above gives
his writing this description?

Foreshadowing

An oft-missed opportunity to layer your story happens by ignoring the
ability to foreshadow via Setting. Narrative Setting description that
evokes emotion can help a reader understand a shift in the mood, as
well as foreshadow what might be coming next. Using Setting this way
can avoid abrupt emotional shifts in the story, where a writer jumps
from one emotion to an opposite one.

EXAMPLE: Paula petted the small kitten, listening to the gentle purr before telling her mother to take a hike.

The passage above is extreme, but as writers we can be so deep into our story we don't see the emotional shifts we're showing the reader.

Foreshadowing via Setting also avoids telling the reader how your character feels, instead of showing how your character feels. Let's see how some authors use the foreshadowing via Setting technique.

Here's a quick sketch of Setting where the POV character drives away from her comfort zone into an unknown environment, but maintains a certain level of security given she's a cop. Do you get a clear sense of where she is emotionally from how she feels about what she sees?

> Merci drove out Modjeska Canyon through the leafless, quivering oaks, her hand tight on the wheel and her eyes fixed on the stripe that seemed to lap out of infinity at her. Black sky, black earth, black road.
>
> —T. Jefferson Parker, *Red Light*

Parker's example shows the emotional state of the POV character through her actions—hand tight on the wheel, eyes fixed on the road—which is then backed up by the Setting description word choices—*leafless, quivering, black, black, black.* He then foreshadows that the reason for her being on this road—to confront a former lover, a fellow cop, and a man she suspects might be a killer—is going to end on an equally bleak note.

The reader is emotionally oriented via the specific Setting details of Modjeska Canyon with its leafless, quivering oaks—a familiarity to those who know Orange County, California, where the story takes place, and a contrast to what most people might think of when they see oaks—usually symbols of strength and steadfastness. Specific adjectives help focus the reader on the emotions the character is feeling—*quivering, tight, black.* This is a very powerful use of Setting deep in a story, since this is the opening to chapter nineteen.

Parker could have had the reader jump from the character in one location into a new scene with her confronting the man. Instead, with two powerful Setting sentences, Parker layers emotion and foreshadowing into the story while transitioning the character through space at the same time.

> **NOTE:** Emotion drives or motivates action in a story. By using Setting to show emotion, the reader is able to understand future actions that come about as a result.

Here's an example from a Young Adult (YA) novel. The POV character, Liesel, is a young girl whose younger brother has died and was recently buried alongside a railroad track somewhere in Germany during the early years of World War II, shortly after the girl's father was arrested as a communist. Now her mother has abandoned the girl, as this was the only way she could give her child a chance of surviving. See how powerfully the author, Markus Zusak, shows the young girl's emotional state, while creating one for the reader, with a few Setting details.

First, let's approach this scene with a hypothetical first-draft version.

> **FIRST DRAFT:** As Liesel sat in the car, she looked out the window at rain clouds but there was no rain.

In this version the reader can see the Setting, but it does not foreshadow anything except the possibility of rain.

> **SECOND DRAFT:** Liesel felt cold and alone as the car drove down the street.

Here the readers are told the emotion of the POV character, but they don't necessarily feel the emotion. Plus there's no Setting shown.

So let's see how Zusak creates a one-two whammy by hinting at the feel of the landscape from the young girl's perspective while he also brings home the emotion of the Setting.

> The day was grey, the color of Europe.

> Curtains were drawn around the car. Liesel made a clear circle
> on the dribbled glass and looked out.
> —Markus Zusak, *The Book Thief*

Every time I read that, my heart aches for this little girl. The author gave the reader a much stronger emotional investment using Setting instead of simply telling us Liesel was sad as the car drove to the home of her new and unknown foster parents.

Let's take this last Setting example and change it up for a different emotional feel.

Here again is the original:

> The day was grey, the color of Europe.
>> Curtains were drawn around the car. Liesel made a clear circle
>> on the dribbled glass and looked out.

Rewritten version showing different emotions:

> The day dawned in sherbet hues of pink and orange.
>> Curtains were tucked around the car windows as Liesel made
>> a clear smiley-face circle on the sparkling glass and peeked out.

What emotions does the second example give you that the first did not? Another rewritten version:

> The sun peeked over the far horizon as if it feared facing the day.
>> Curtains hunkered tight against the closed car windows. Liesel
>> ached to make a handprint on the dribbled glass but was lashed into
>> her seatbelt and couldn't reach anything.

Can you see how the Setting word choices in the rewrites are very different from the original?

NOTE: Determine the emotional mood of a passage before you write it, or during your revision process, to ramp up your use of Setting.

Here's another powerful Setting description. The POV character is following up a lead on the whereabouts of a paranormal threat. She is traveling down a familiar country road near the town where she lives on the
way to a confrontation. These are her thoughts as she notices the Setting
around her. Do you get a sense of the emotional state of the character by
what she sees and how she thinks of the Setting?

> Grapevines, bare in their winter guise, lined the wall. In the moon-
> light they looked like a row of dead men, hanging arms spread wide
> and crucified on the frames that supported them.
> —Patricia Briggs, *Moon Called*

The Setting above not only orients the reader to the change from one
environment—the city of Richland, where the story takes place—to the
outlying farm area, but it also deepens the readers' experience of what
the character is feeling. The author sets an emotional tone with the use
of key words: *bare, dead men, arms spread wide, crucified*. What if Briggs
had chosen to streamline her Setting description?

> **ROUGH DRAFT:** As Mercy Thompson drove from Richland
> through the farmland, she noticed the grapevines which hadn't
> sprouted yet.

Whole different emotional feel, isn't it?

One more example to show it doesn't take a lot of words in a Setting
description to get the emotional feel of a passage across.

> In the distance, cypresses rose, their bloated trunks grotesquely
> fat, like old men with beer guts squatting in the mud. Sunrise was
> due in half an hour, and the sky and the water glowed the pale gray
> of a worn-out dime.
> —Ilona Andrews, *Bayou Moon*

Only two sentences, but the reader feels the threat of the location and
the feel of the day.

Reinforcing Story Themes

Setting and how the character interacts with it are great ways to reinforce the themes in your story. By using contrasting reactions between characters and the Setting, and contrasting emotions, awkwardness, or confidence in a character's interaction with a Setting, you can highlight a story's theme.

In the Setting passage below, the POV character realizes the love affair she's been having with a priest is making her terribly unhappy. A secondary character, a man who knew her years ago and recently met her again, has shared that he always thought of her as focused, one-dimensional, and pretty straight-laced. These words enhance her feelings that she always played it safe, was never spontaneous, and maybe missed out a lot on life.

Watch how Tess Gerritsen uses a long Setting description to show a life rigidly controlled and focused on work, versus a life of spontaneity and joy. We experience the passage from the POV of Maura Isles, a character who lives in Boston and is familiar with winter and snow. Here she views snow in Wyoming by watching how secondary characters react to an unexpected snowfall. The Setting gives a hint of who the secondary characters are by how they react to the Setting, and the emotional feel gives a motivation for the POV character's decision to take an unexpected trip—one with deadly results.

> During the night, it had started to snow, and by the time they loaded their luggage into the back of the Suburban, three inches of white fluff coated the cars in the parking lot, a pristine cloak that made the San Diego contingent ooh and ahh at the beauty of it. Doug and Arlo insisted on taking photos of the three ladies posed in front of the hotel entrance, everyone smiling and rosy-cheeked in their ski clothes. Snow was nothing new for Maura, but she saw it now the way these Californians did, with a sense of wonder at how clean and white it was, how softly it settled on her eyelashes, how silent it swirled from the sky. During Boston's long winters, snow meant

tiresome shoveling and wet boots and slushy streets. It was merely a fact of life that had to be dealt with until spring. But this snow felt different; it was vacation snow, and she smiled at the sky, feeling as giddy as her companions, enchanted by a world that suddenly looked new and bright.

—Tess Gerritsen, *Ice Cold*

This is a great example of using Setting to show emotion. Notice it's completely active and doesn't slow the forward momentum of the story. We are engaged in the shifting realizations and emotions of the POV character. Now let's dig into it to see how this passage reinforces the story theme that premeditation or careful planning in your life can have negative consequences, just as spontaneous, poorly thought-out actions can.

During the night, it had started to snow, and by the time they loaded their luggage into the back of the Suburban, three inches of white fluff [*Specific word choice.*] coated the cars in the parking lot, a pristine cloak [*Specific word choices continuing the idea of snow as a nice thing.*] that made the San Diego contingent ooh and ahh at the beauty [*Showing followed by a telling explanation.*] of it. [*Here Gerritsen could simply have stated that it had snowed and how much since the previous night. But by adding that the secondary characters loved the beauty of the snow, which is in direct contrast to the POV character's emotional mood up to this point, the reader gets to experience the story on a deeper level. The emotional contrast is between the character, previously called focused and one-dimensional in her calculated approach to life, and the actions of the secondary characters, who are reveling in the unexpected.*] Doug and Arlo insisted on taking photos of the three ladies posed in front of the hotel entrance, everyone smiling and rosy-cheeked in their ski clothes. [*And here the addition of the words rosy-cheeked is a nice detail that anyone who has been around chilling temperatures knows very well. Plus it's a word choice that evokes positive, happy emotions.*] Snow was nothing new for Maura, but she saw it now the way these Californians did, with a sense of wonder at how clean and white it was, how softly it settled on her eyelashes, how silent it swirled from the sky. [*More positive descriptive words. Gerritsen also reveals to the reader that the POV character is familiar with snow, which readers of the series already know, but then she follows up this telling with showing and contrasting in the next sentence. The close third-person POV directly reacting to the Setting makes it clear to the reader that the Setting is mirroring her emotional state and the theme of the novel.*] During Boston's long winters, snow meant tiresome shoveling and wet boots and slushy streets. [*Different specific word choices to show snow in a very different light.*] It was merely a fact of life that had to be dealt with until spring. But this snow felt different; it was vacation snow, and she smiled at the sky, feeling as giddy as her companions, enchanted by a world that suddenly looked new and bright. [*Lovely contrast between where the POV character was when the story opened (unhappy) and her current emotional response (delighted, charmed, engaged). This indicates that this venture is meant to be fun, which is very different from Maura's everyday world. As the story progresses, the reader will see that Maura is throwing herself into the spontaneity of the moment by agreeing to go on this unplanned road trip, which will create unexpected consequences. This reflects that people need to find balance in their lives, rather than an all-or-nothing reaction.*]

Gerritsen effectively uses Setting as a symbol here. She uses place and the movement through place as a metaphor for the character's emotional growth and change. At the beginning of the story, Maura is in Boston—unhappy, because of a no-win romantic relationship and her focus on work. Winter is approaching and her Setting is gray, growing cold, and shutting down seasonally. This echoes her life.

She travels to Wyoming on business, which affords her a spur-of-the-moment trip to a ski resort, a journey that is very out of character for the nonspontaneous Maura. The passage above is a metaphor for how this change opens up Maura's emotions and lightens her sense of who she is through Setting. When an unexpected accident occurs and she is stranded in the wilds of Wyoming—where the average population density is one person for every 5.5 square miles versus Boston's 13,041 people per square mile—the Setting once again highlights how physically and emotionally isolated the character is.

By the end of the story, after her life-threatening and harrowing stay in Wyoming, Maura sees her hometown, her world, and her relationships in a very different light, much of which is shown emotionally via Setting descriptions. The story's theme of finding balance is achieved.

> **NOTE:** Using emotional contrast in describing a Setting can be a very effective way of showing the reader that the POV character is now in a different state emotionally than earlier or later in your story.

What Not to Do

- Don't shift the emotional tone of a scene too abruptly.
- Don't forget to include emotion on the page.
- Don't forget that emotion creates motivation for a character's actions.
- Do not tell without also showing.
- Remember that emotion can foreshadow a change in a character's perceptions, and thus the readers' perceptions.
- Don't be vague and inconsistent in your story theme.
- Never be too vague or general in your choice of descriptive terms when the Setting matters to the story. A *large lake* says little to a reader unless they know what you, as the writer, mean by *large*.

Assignment

Take the following situational prompt:

> Sue is driving down a road in her hometown.

Pretty generic, yes? Now add Setting and rewrite the prompt any way you wish in order to show the following:

- An excited Sue
- A scared Sue
- A resigned Sue
- A frustrated Sue

See if you can write tight and focused sentences—no more than three to four. Focus on what Sue might see and feel about what she sees around her, given her different emotional states. Have fun!

OR: Look at your own WIP. Find a Setting that's currently devoid of emotion. Can you focus in and see any ways to add emotion to what you currently have on the page? Look to thread through your emotionally charged words, action verbs, and details with what you currently have, without adding too many words to the passage.

Recap

- Readers read for the emotion of the story.
- Power up those verbs to get more emotion into a Setting description. Don't rely solely on your adjectives.
- Active Setting can set the mood or theme of a story emotionally, which makes it easier for the reader to accept what is unfolding or about to unfold.
- Show, don't tell, the emotion by showing how the character views and feels about the Setting.
- Use concrete images and consistent, specific word choices to describe your Setting.
- Determine the emotional mood of a passage either before you write it or during your revision process, to ramp up your use of Setting.

05

Using Setting to Create Complication

Once we start to see the power of using Setting, it's difficult to go back to simply stringing descriptive words together without looking at them critically. In this chapter we'll go a bit deeper and look at how to use Setting to show conflict or complications in a character's world through word choices. This will also show how to focus a reader on what's happening for the character.

Let's look at a master of Setting, Barbara Kingsolver:

> The cluttered kitchen irritates her. The Formica countertop is patterned with pink and black loops like rubber bands lying against each other, getting on her nerves, all cocked and ready to spring like hail across the kitchen. Alice wonders if other women in the middle of the night have begun to resent their Formica. She stares hard at the telephone on the counter, wishing it would ring. She needs some proof that she isn't the last woman left on earth, the surviving queen of nothing. The clock gulps softly, eating seconds whole while she waits; receives no proof.
> —Barbara Kingsolver, *Pigs in Heaven*

The above example clearly shows the POV character's emotions, but let's pull it apart to see the tension and conflict at play in this Setting description.

The cluttered kitchen irritates her. [*Look at the adjective and active verb here. This is not a woman who is in love with her home. Her growing awareness of dissatisfaction in her life is shown, not told, through her view of her kitchen, a room very often associated with the heart of a home.*] The Formica countertop is patterned with pink and black loops like rubber bands lying against each other, getting on her nerves, all cocked and ready to spring like hail across the kitchen. [*If the author stopped at the pattern it would still be a good visual, but she took the description one more step by describing what those squiggles mean to the character—an image that's tense and poised for change.*] Alice wonders if other women in the middle of the night have begun to resent their Formica. [*Telling that enhances, instead of replaces, the previous showing elements.*] She stares hard at the telephone on the counter, wishing it would ring. She needs some proof that she isn't the last woman left on earth, the surviving queen of nothing. The clock gulps [*Wonderful action verb that also gives a strong sensory image.*] softly, eating seconds whole while she waits; receives no proof. [*This last sentence alone is fresh but it still shows how this woman feels about her life. Kingsolver's word choices, and the choices of what to focus on in Alice's kitchen, highlight the conflict between where Alice is now and her yearning to be or feel something different. This feeling, in turn, sends her off on her story journey.*]

This is where what you learned about weaving emotion into your Settings in the last chapter can be taken a step further. A gray day can simply be a gray day, or the rain can become a nuisance as a character runs from one location to another without an umbrella. But if you have a character who is experiencing dissatisfaction, which in turn sets her up to make a decision or act in a way that will complicate her life, using Setting to build or to foreshadow that conflict can be extremely effective.

Foreshadowing Trouble or Conflict via Setting

Let's see how author Dennis Lehane foreshadows upcoming complications. In this short passage the POV character is moving from point A to point B, where he's due for a job interview. It's a job he really doesn't want to take, but feels he has no choice. Watch how the author makes that clear by noting what the character sees and how he describes the Setting with details.

> On the walk to the subway, I drank my cup of Dunkin's under a low, clay sky and ragged clouds. Brittle gray leaves stirred in the gutter, waiting to fossilize in the first snow. The trees were bare along Crescent Avenue, and cold air off the ocean hunted the gaps in my clothes.
>
> —Dennis Lehane, *Moonlight Mile*

A less-experienced writer might have rushed the character to the job interview and focused on using anticipation and internalization to show conflict. Lehane sets readers up emotionally so we know how this character feels, shows his resistance, and brings it home by his word choices—*low, clay sky, ragged clouds, brittle gray leaves, stirred in the gutter, fossilize, bare trees, cold air, hunted the gaps in his clothes.* These are not the observations of a man excited with his world or feeling optimistic about taking a nine-to-five job in corporate security.

> **NOTE:** Once you start using Active Setting, you'll quickly find yourself combining the elements we're studying in this book to create maximum effect without adding a lot of additional words.

The next example includes emotion and foreshadowing, both of which ramp up the conflict in the story.

But first, let's look at a possible rough draft

FIRST DRAFT: I drove down the dark road toward the crime scene.

The destination raises a story question, but the rest of the sentence isn't working hard enough. Let's see how Laurell K. Hamilton not only transitions her character from one location to the other, but also ratchets up the sense of conflict in the passage.

> The trees curled over the road, naked branches bouncing in the headlight. Wet, icy trunks bent towards the road. In the summertime the road would be a leafy tunnel, now it was just black bones erupting from the white snow.
> —Laurell K. Hamilton, *The Lunatic Café*

Do you get the stronger sense of impending trouble or danger? Hamilton doesn't wait until the crime scene to show that things are going to get worse for this POV character; instead she leads the reader to that point step by step.

The author of this next example does the same thing in a different mystery. In this passage the POV character has tracked down the meeting location of a local AA group. He needs to find people within this building who might know something about a murder victim and a motivation for her death. The group is known to be reluctant to talk about what happens in their meetings, because that easily erodes the level of trust that is painstakingly built between them. The reader already knows this. A less-intentional writer might have jumped from that information reveal via dialogue straight to interviewing the members, which will show more conflict. But an opportunity would have been lost. Let's see how Louise Penny did not simply rely on dialogue for conflict, but enhanced it through the inspector's observations of his Setting.

> Chief Inspector Gamache stood on rue Sherbrooke, in downtown Montreal, and stared at the heavy, red brick church across the street. It wasn't made with bricks so much as huge, rectangular ox blood stones. He'd passed it hundreds of times while driving and never really looked at it.
>
> But now he did.

It was dark and ugly and uninviting. It didn't shout salvation.
Didn't even whisper it. What it did shout was penance and atonement. Guilt and punishment.

It looked like a prison for sinners. Few would enter with an
easy step and light heart.

—Louise Penny, *A Trick of the Light*

Pulling out the specific Setting details might make the conflict clearer.
As you read the key sentences, ask yourself: Does this look like the kind
of place, foreshadowing the people who meet for mutual support within,
that will give a murder investigator answers?

It wasn't made with bricks so much as huge, rectangular ox blood stones.

It was dark and ugly and uninviting. It didn't shout salvation.
Didn't even whisper it. What it did shout was penance and atonement. Guilt and punishment.

It looked like a prison for sinners.

Powerful, specific, descriptive, and focused images—*huge, rectangular
ox blood*; *dark and ugly and uninviting*—add to the character's
interpretation of what he's seeing—*penance and atonement*; *guilt and
punishment*; *a prison for sinners*.

What the author did was use Setting in combination with interpretation of that Setting. It's a powerful one-two combination that leads
the reader to expect exactly what the author wants them to expect—
impending conflict and complication.

This next example shows the conflict between the POV character,
a mother whose daughter has been committed to a psychiatric evalua-
tion home by the daughter's husband, and the psychiatrist treating the
daughter. The mother feels that the husband is actively working against
her daughter, and if her daughter remains at the home, she will be in
danger. The mother has arrived at the home hoping to communicate
with the resident psychiatrist who is friends with the husband. See how
the author, Emilie Richards, imparts this conflict through Setting:

He led her down the hallway to the door he'd come through. His office was much as she expected. Leather furniture, dark paneled walls covered with multiple framed diplomas, a desk as massive as a psychiatrist's ego. She always wondered if professional men measured the size of their desks the way adolescent boys measured their penises.

—Emilie Richards, *Fox River*

The reader is given a few key words of description, but most of the Setting is translated through the mother's POV. Thus the reader knows exactly how she feels about the man keeping her from her daughter, based on what she sees of his personal space.

What if Richards had chosen simply to describe the office space?

> **ROUGH DRAFT:** Leather furniture, dark paneled walls covered with multiple framed diplomas, a massive desk.

The above description is so generic as to be almost invisible. So let's look more closely at how Richards enhanced the generic to show the reader that the POV character knew getting her daughter away from the psychiatrist was not going to be easy, just by seeing his office.

> He led her down the hallway to the door he'd come through. [*Not much Setting description here, but this line transitions the reader from one space to another and shows the reader that the male psychiatrist is in charge by forcing the mother to follow him to his space.*] His office was much as she expected. [*Telling, which if left on its own, would not place the reader deep into the passage, but does set the reader up to understand the space more.*] Leather furniture, dark paneled walls covered with multiple framed diplomas, [*Through this reveal we have generic Setting with a hint of ego revealed by the number of diplomas shown.*] a desk as massive as a psychiatrist's ego. [*Bam, right here, by using the piece of furniture to show something about the psychiatrist, this room comes alive.*] She always wondered if professional men measured the size of their desks the way adolescent boys measured their penises. [*The image of that*

massive desk is followed by a very scathing observation that leaves
the reader no doubt about the emotional subtext in this passage.
The POV character is not intimidated, impressed, or cowed, but she
is aware that she's dealing with a man in power. By using Setting so
skillfully, Richards has alerted the reader to the tension and conflict
between the characters.]

Internal and Emotional Conflict

Setting is a wonderful way to show a character's emotional or internal
conflict. By showing how your POV character interacts with a Setting,
and using descriptive words to bring that to the fore, you can reveal how
that character is feeling at that moment about himself, the people he is
interacting with, and even his world. Emotion drives action in your story, so by using Setting to show internal or emotional conflict, you create
the motivation for that character's next actions.

If you are a fan of TV dramas, have you ever noticed how the film-
ing of a scene, using gritty details such as darkness, graffiti, strewn garbage, and crumbling buildings helps increase the sense of danger and
tension? The Setting is intentionally used to enhance the conflict that's
about to unfold. In a visual context, such as a TV drama, the emotion
is often revealed by the music, dialogues, situations, and, of course, the
Setting. The writer has to use those same cues for the reader to help her
intentionally experience the elements the author wants her to. Conflict
is one of those elements.

Here we'll go back again to see how Jamie Ford shows internal or
emotional conflict through his *New York Times'* bestseller *Hotel on the
Corner of Bitter and Sweet*. It is forty years after the POV character, Henry Lee, was separated from his childhood friend and first love when her
family was interred in the Japanese resettlement camps of WWII. Now
Henry discovers that her family's belongings, which had been stored for
decades, have been uncovered. We'll see his first visit to the basement
storage facility. Take note how the author skillfully shows more than a

simple walk into the basement, a movement through space. By his specific use of details in the Setting, the author illuminates the internal or emotional conflict Henry feels about what he is about to discover and how that discovery means digging up other buried memories.

But before we get to Ford's words, let's create a rough draft.

> **FIRST DRAFT:** Henry went into the basement to see the items left by the Japanese who had been resettled.

Not much internal conflict here. We simply have a character moving from point A to point B in the story.

> **SECOND DRAFT:** Henry went down a dark stairwell, through a thick door that opened on creaking hinges. The door was a subbasement beneath the old hotel itself. It was lit by utility bulbs.

In this second version, the reader can see more of what Henry sees and gets a small hint of emotional feeling for the Setting. But there's no sense of how deeply Henry feels about this space and its meaning. Nor about how his interaction with this Setting creates so much emotional or internal discord within him—the same emotions that send him off on both an internal and external story journey.

So let's look at how Jamie Ford imbues the passage below with emotional conflict.

> **NOTE:** Be careful of creating a pattern of adjective-noun-verb, adjective-noun-verb, as in the previous draft. The reader can pick up on that pattern very quickly, and it can pull them out of the story.

> Henry headed down a paint-chipped stairwell, through a thick wooden door that opened on creaking hinges. The door spilled into a large expanse of subbasement beneath the old hotel itself. The only illumination came from a handful of utility bulbs, hung like Christmas tree lights along the ceiling by large staples; a long trail of bright orange extension cord led the way.
> —Jamie Ford, *Hotel on the Corner of Bitter and Sweet*

A Writer's Guide to Active Setting

In this passage the reader is shown the conflict Henry Lee feels in this visit to not just any place, but a place that echoes with the past—where mistakes were made, promises given, and regrets linger. The writer understands how to use Setting to reveal that this place matters to a character because of his past. Ford does not tell the reader this; he shows the reader with a metaphoric and literal journey down into darkness, with the ending note of Christmas-tree lights, usually a happy image used to contrast with the previous images—*paint-chipped, creaking hinges, old, subbasement*. The lights let us grab on to a small element of hope, but not much.

In the next example, from a paranormal romance novel with the pacing sensibilities of a romantic suspense, the heroine sees for the first time where her client and love interest lives. He's been arrested for illegal cage fighting, and she's his court-appointed attorney, so there's already conflict built into the relationship. But the author doesn't stop there. She adds in the internal conflict, the emotional reasons that can make finding and acknowledging love so hard. In this case, it's class differences. He comes from a hardscrabble background and goes into an elite, and very shadowy Special Forces group where dying is the only way out. She comes from a privileged and well-connected upper-crust Boston family. She does not see the class distinctions as an obstacle as much as he does, and these short and focused sentences bring home that point very well. Even though we're in her point of view, it's easier to understand where he's coming from, and both the reader, and the POV character, learn why he feels conflict.

> The old pine floors had all the gloss of a sheet of sandpaper, and the ceiling had water stains in the corners that were the color of urine. No furniture in sight, not one table or chair or TV. Just a sleeping bag, a pair of combat boots and some clothes in precisely folded piles.
>
> Isaac Rothe's pillow was nothing but a sweatshirt.
>
> —J.R. Ward, *Crave*

What if the author had trusted that the reader would accept the class distinction conflict as revealed by his internalizations alone? Like this:

> **ROUGH DRAFT:** I went to the shabby room that Isaac Roth rented and got a better idea of why he felt out of his league getting together with me.

The reader is being asked to wait in this version. They're being told, not shown, and the passage does nothing to deepen or reveal the conflict. Many writers stop at this point, but not the strongest writers.

Here's a subtle example of emotional/internal conflict shown, step by step, by how the POV character sees the Setting around him. He's uncharacteristically gone out of his way for the sake of a woman he barely knows and has agreed to meet her at a bus stop to drive her home. See if you can grasp how he feels about his action.

> By two o'clock the clouds had given up their roiling and simply sat down on the land, transforming the rain into a gray fog. It was like a cold steam room and it pinned in place every odor. The Major was still screwing up his nose against the ripe smell of urine long after a wandering collie dog had left his mark on the corner post of the wooden bus shed. The rough three-sided wooden shed with its cheap asphalt roof offered no protection from the fog and leached its own smell of creosote and old vomit into the dampness. The Major cursed the human instinct for shelter that made him stand under it.
>
> —Helen Simonson, *Major Pettigrew's Last Stand*

The character is not very happy about the situation he's in, based on his own actions, is he? This example of Setting reinforces where the character is internally at the beginning of the story and is used as a contrast for later when he begins to grow and change.

To further explore this concept, here is another example of conflict revealed through Setting, this one from a thriller author, Elmore Leonard. Look closely at how the POV character, Bobby, gives the reader a sense of a different secondary character as he views the woman's home. Through Bobby's internalization—his emotional response to the Setting he sees— he gets a strong sense that he and this unknown woman will be butting heads. Elmore brings the reader so deep into the POV character's street-hardened thought process that the upcoming conflict between what Bobby wants and what other characters want is highlighted even more.

> What Bobby was thinking now, watching the fortune-teller's house, there could be a problem with her. He knew it without knowing the woman. Felt it looking at the house, the vegetation almost hiding it: an old melaleuca rotting inside itself, palmettos that had never been cut back growing wild across the front windows. A woman who lived alone in a house like that had problems. And a woman with problems, man, could make you have some of your own.
> —Elmore Leonard, *Riding the Rap*

The woman is young, attractive, and sensual, and, if the first description of her focuses solely on how she looks, there's no conflict. But here, by seeing an impression of her as a person who has problems, conflict is foreshadowed. The reader is introduced to the woman here through her surroundings. But by having the reader first encounter an image of where she lives, which contrasts with how she looks, it foreshadows subtle emotional conflict for Bobby before he meets her. The author uses telling, then showing, to make it clear to the reader in one paragraph that this woman is going to cause story complications.

Conflict and World Building

For writers of fantasy, urban fantasy, steampunk, science fiction, and dystopian novels, the world of the story is, many times, completely fabricated. This means the Setting can be unique and never seen, anywhere, by anyone. While that can sound like an easy way to write whatever you want, it can cause pitfalls because the reader can be cast adrift from your story, with no reference points to see where the characters are interacting. So while unique Setting is vital in these kinds of stories, your reader needs to be anchored by that Setting quickly and easily. Then he can focus on other elements of your story, such as the conflict, which is just as critical.

We'll examine how one science fiction/fantasy writer accomplishes this feat in a short passage, but before we do that, let's assume the author skipped Setting details altogether. After all, this scene happens late in the story, and shouldn't the reader have an idea of what the world is like on this planet by now? Yes and no.

Anytime you change a scene, open a new chapter, or want to ramp up what you've already started on the page, that is the time to use Setting to work harder. In this next example the author was showing how two characters were drawing closer to one another, creating a relationship that would not be easy for either. Two characters on a planet called Madrid, one of whom is leaving soon and the other who has professed a vow of chastity in her role as a nun, find themselves attracted to each other and conflicted about it. The author could have written:

> **FIRST DRAFT:** After driving around the empty spaces of the planet for a while, he stopped the hovercraft, very aware that whatever was between them was as yet unresolved.

This is where newer writers might think—*good enough*—and jump into dialogue, showing the reader the turmoil and challenges keeping these two from committing to one another. But the author will use dialogue, right after she enhances what's happening internally—the conflict—by the view of where they are externally. The woman, who is from this planet, has taken the man, who is an outsider, to her favorite spot. We're in his POV as they walk to a specific point.

> The thin metal railing did not seem like much protection between them and the rocky gorse below, white and sharp as teeth in the milky moonlight. It was the highest point in all Madrid, and the city stretched before them like a black cat sprinkled with diamonds.
> —Sharon Shinn, *Wrapt in Crystal*

Let's take apart this passage to see exactly how it leads a reader into believing there is attraction, and conflict, between the two characters.

> The thin metal railing did not seem like much protection between them and the rocky gorse below, [*This is a metaphor for the emotional state of each character—each feels vulnerable and unprotected.*] white and sharp as teeth in the milky moonlight. [*Fresh imagery showing not only the rocky drop, but an emotional response—the image is not left on the sharp rocks, but softened by the ending phrase, in the milky moonlight, which softens and adds a gentle tone here. There isn't danger, so much as a hard choice that could offer either danger or the opposite.*] It was the highest point in all Madrid, [*Simply a telling detail but because going to the highest point of a mountain is often a reference to enlightenment and clarity, this foreshadows what might happen between the two.*] and the city stretched before them like a black cat sprinkled with diamonds. [*This fresh imagery leaves the description on a positive note. Nothing is resolved between these two, but at this point the reader believes the relationship could still evolve, in spite of the dangers.*]

NOTE: You can transition a reader from one emotion to another by starting on one emotional note and ending on the opposite, which raises a question in the reader's mind as to what the outcome will be.

Orientation and Conflict

Setting is important for orienting the reader to time and place as you move your characters through your story. But digging deeper as a writer and using Setting to ratchet up conflict can be a strong tool as you get the reader to focus on a character's clear responses to a place. It allows you to orient the reader as to where she is, and to reveal a lot about the character, as well as what might be happening, or about to happen, in the story.

In this first example, the POV character, an Army Military Police Investigator has arrived at the scene of the suspicious death of a high-ranking General. By taking the time to orient the reader to the crime scene, the reader is able to understand a little more about what this character is going up against in investigating the death. The investigator has already determined that the motel (where the death occurred) rented rooms by the hour and the room was paid in cash, so there's little help there. Now he's stepped outside to see what's around him.

> There was a no-name cinder-block lounge bar with lots of neon
> and no windows. It had an Exotic Dancers sign lit up in pink and
> a parking lot the size of a football field.
> —Lee Child, *The Enemy*

This is a small, short passage that expands the conflict already set up by the lack of witnesses at the motel. Look at the word choices—*cinder block lounge bar* and *no windows*. Then, by adding a visual of what type of bar it is—*Exotic Dancers sign lit up in pink*—the likelihood that there are witnesses who would be focused on anything but the bar and the dancers isn't good. Two sentences and the author has ratcheted up the conflict of finding witnesses to a suspicious death.

Here's a Setting example, early in a story that not only anchors the reader as to where the story is unfolding, but foreshadows upcoming conflict by contrasting the image of the city, as viewed by the POV character, with what's already happened.

At this point, the POV character has just returned from the funeral of a good friend, a woman who died of AIDS contracted from a blood transfusion. When she reaches the dead woman's house, she runs into a group of protestors using the situation as an anti-AIDS rally. The POV character reflects on the people she sees and the town she's in:

> They thought Santa Barbara, this postcard city of acrylic blue skies
> and red tile roofs, of coffee bars and beaches and Mexican Ameri-

can warmth, was a sluice gate on the sewer pipe to hell. They liked
to drive home the point by jeering at AIDS funerals.
—Meg Gardiner, *China Lake*

The idyllic setting is twisted back upon itself with one short, stirring sentence. This city may look like paradise on one level, but there's a lot more going on. Talk about a strong one-two conflict punch, all relayed through Setting.

Here's how another author gives the reader a hint of backstory and more than a hint of conflict as the POV character returns to his childhood home for the funeral of his father:

When people give directions to any home or business on West Covington, they use our house as a negative landmark; if you see the big white house, then you've gone too far. Which is precisely what I'm thinking as I pull into the driveway.
—Jonathan Tropper, *This Is Where I Leave You*

The reader isn't given a visual image of a large white mini-mansion with Doric columns and delusions of grandeur. Instead, by combining place with the POV character's specific response, the story conflict and unfolding story drama is succinctly foreshadowed and shown, not simply told.

> **NOTE:** Using Setting to highlight conflict can be a powerful device. Use a character's positive or negative response to a place to reveal to the reader a lot about the character and a lot about what might be happening, or about to happen, in the story.

Here's another example from an old classic by Ngaio Marsh. By opening a mystery story set on an ocean-going ship, the author creates a closed-room mystery. She foreshadows the conflict by contrasting the POV of a minor secondary character, a police constable who is not on board, to introduce the Setting. This police officer, walking his beat, foreshadows the contrast between the idyllic belief that an ocean voyage is very attractive and desirable, and the upcoming reality of what can happen when a small group of strangers becomes trapped in a small environment with an unknown killer.

But before we get to Marsh's prose, let's look at how she might have built her words to maximize the Setting details.

> **FIRST DRAFT:** The police constable stood on the dock and looked at the ship moored there.

The reader gets a vague idea of a ship waiting to sail. Not much here and certainly no sense of impending conflict.

> **SECOND DRAFT:** The hour was late as the police constable walked his beat, thinking how he'd like to sail away on the ship waiting at the dock to leave.

In this draft, there's a hint of conflict between what the constable wants and what he is doing, but this was not the author's intention. Marsh's intention was to show one setting, the dockside where the constable is on his rounds, and the more romantic world of a ship about to embark on a cruise. In and of itself this does not imply conflict, only the contrast between what he thinks the ship represents and what it will become. This is where the tension, the conflict, is shown. Let's see how Ngaio Marsh uses Setting to foreshadow conflict.

> Police Constable Moir, on duty until midnight, walked in and out of shadows. He breathed the soft cold smell of wet wood and heard the slap of the night tide against the wharves. Acres and acres of shipping and forests of cranes lay around him. Ships, he thought romantically, were, in a sort of way, like little worlds. Tied up to bollards and lying quiet enough but soon to sail over the watery globe as lonely as the planets wandering in the skies.
> —Ngaio Marsh, *Singing in the Shrouds*

Did you get the wonderful sensory details Marsh employs in the setting? The atmospheric details, the wistful sense of intrigue one has when thinking about a voyage from the perspective of a person trapped in the

A Writer's Guide to Active Setting

routine of his nightly rounds, these serve to heighten the sense of impending conflict, all in four sentences of Setting. The reader is in the scene, but this dockside vignette is not simply to show a cop on his beat. It uses this POV character to show the reader subtext by using specific word choices—*in and out of shadows, little worlds, watery globe, lonely*. What if Marsh had skipped these and her other word choices?

> **ROUGH DRAFT:** The cop looked at the ship waiting to sail and wondered what it would be like to take a trip.

Ho hum. No emotion here. No conflict. No contrast used to punch up the sense of impending danger being raised in the reader's mind. A waste of a great opportunity.

Conflict via Contrast

A quick and easy way to create tension, or conflict, on the page is by using contrast. If a Setting is beautiful, you can create one set of emotions and reader expectations about what's going to happen as a result of the character in this Setting. But if the Setting is both beautiful and ugly, then a question is raised in the reader's mind as to what's about to happen. Tension drives the pacing of your story. A nifty way to show, not tell, inherent tension in your story is by using Setting, and contrast within it, to alert the reader.

In this first example we're looking through the POV of a young man who is resorting to illegal cage fighting as a quick way to make a buck and stay below the radar of very powerful and dangerous men tracking him (see the earlier J.R. Ward example). He's already been arrested, and is out on bail. He knows he needs to disappear now, but he's lost all his funds posting bail. So he decides to participate in one more fight. He arrives at the event's location, seeing the Setting for the first time. The character is used to these events being held in less-than-welcoming places, but this one is in a nearly-finished set of office buildings that look posh and finished on the outside, but are raw and empty on the inside. This reflects how he's feeling. Then he spots where he's going to fight.

Before we jump to the author's version, which shows conflict via the contrast between the external location and where this man must fight, let's assume an early draft was written.

> **FIRST DRAFT:** Isaac Roth was impressed by the vaulted ceilings and floor-to-ceiling windows of the unfinished office complex. It was nice—too bad it wasn't finished.

In this version, the focus is on how the POV character feels about one aspect of the Setting. Not only is there no contrast, there's no tension, no sense of impending conflict. The two sentences are all about what's working, and nothing about what isn't working or might cause trouble for the character.

> **SECOND DRAFT:** The cage where he was about to fight looked like all the other cages in which he'd fought for his life.

The focus on this second attempt shows the reader nothing, leaving her to wonder what the cage is or why being in one should cause problems. It's a classic case of the writer assuming there's more on the page than there actually is. As written, all the reader has is the word "cage," which leaves it up to her to guess what that means. As a result, there's not a lot of conflict.

So let's see how author J.R. Ward brings the Setting to life, and through it ramps up the conflict, because the reader has no doubt why stepping in this "cage," that's so very different than the ritzy, if unfinished, location, is dangerous.

> Tonight's poor-man's MGM Grand was about sixty thousand square feet of cold air anchored by concrete floor and four walls' worth of dirty windows. The "octagon" was set up in the far corner, the eight-sided ring bolted in and surprisingly sturdy.
> —J.R. Ward, *Crave*

Now we have contrast—*poor-man's MGM Grand*. In other words, the front of the building was for one type of person, but where the fight would take place was another world. He's stepping into cold air, not because he's too warm and it's welcoming but because the space is huge—*sixty-thousand square feet of huge*—with the cage, called the "octagon," bolted in and sturdy. Now the reader is clearly shown what this man has to face even before he meets his opponent within that anchored trap.

Here's another short but powerful Setting description that not only foreshadows conflict based on the contrasts noted, but reveals a lot about the POV character's emotions as he thinks about where he is.

> Cannery Row in Monterey in California is a poem, a stink, a grating
> noise, a quality of light, a tone, a habit, a nostalgia, a dream.
> —John Steinbeck, *Cannery Row*

By using contrasting images to paint the city, Steinbeck shows the reader that people in this specific part of town have different expectations and different experiences. And where differences rub shoulders there's bound to be conflict eventually. Note also how Steinbeck starts and ends his Setting description on two positive images—*a poem, a dream*. By bracketing the description this way, Steinbeck makes it clear that the POV character is attracted to Cannery Row in spite of its negative elements. If Steinbeck had swapped his words around he would have transitioned the reader from a positive feel to a negative one:

> **REWRITTEN:** Cannery Row in Monterey in California is a poem,
> a dream, a quality of light, a nostalgia, a tone, a habit, a grating
> noise, a stink.

NOTE: Bracketing positive or negative word choices with their opposites will show how the POV character truly feels about a Setting and can set up conflict. However, starting a Setting description with specific word choices and ending on opposite word choices shows a transition from one feeling to another, but does not necessarily show conflict. Tension is resolved when the description ends on a decisive note as in the Steinbeck example.

Let's next look at how one author uses contrast between two principal characters in his story to heighten their differences, and thus the conflict between them, as they find themselves in the same Setting at the same time but with very different POVs.

First, from the antagonist's POV: The reader already knows this man is at odds with the protagonist, but the author reinforces that in the following passages.

> He lay wide awake in his tent as the light from the fire danced its fingers against the canvas. The ground was hard and lumpy. The air was so cold he could see his breath. And, all around him, wild beasts reminded him that he was invading their territory.
> —Colin Cotterill, *Curse of the Pogo Stick*

Now we shift to the protagonist's POV. Compare what you learn about him because you've already been introduced to the Setting above.

> December in the mountains of Xiang Khouang was too cold and high for mosquitoes. Siri slept in a hammock slung between two sturdy breast fruit trees. Wrapped in a blanket, he smiled up at the stars that extended from horizon to horizon. He breathed in the scents: the night orchids that hid their beauty shyly during the day and blossomed under moonlight, the release sourness plants, and the sudden love vegetables. He listened to jungle music: the choir of birds and beasts that sang through the night. The air was so fresh he could feel his insides waking from a long polluted hibernation.
> —Colin Cotterill, *Curse of the Pogo Stick*

Let's pull these two examples apart to see how Cotterill ratchets up conflict not only by using Setting, but by using contrasting POVs to show Setting.

He lay wide awake [*A hint here that though the man went to bed, he's not yet asleep. The reader doesn't know if this is a good thing or not.*] in his tent as the light from the fire danced its fingers against the canvas. [*Fresh description that lets us know he's inside a tent.*] The ground was hard and lumpy. The air was so cold he could see his breath. [*Sensory details revealed as negative.*] And, all around him, wild beasts reminded him that he was invading their territory. [*Shows characterization by his response to the Setting. Compare this to the next passage of another character in this same place, same trip, same everything—except how he sees the Setting.*]

December in the mountains of Xiang Khouang was too cold and high for mosquitoes. [*Orients the reader as to time of year and location, but also lets the reader know this man thinks of the mountains in a specific way. The mountains are not some vague general unknown, but a place he knows.*] Siri slept in a hammock slung between two sturdy breast fruit trees. [*Specific details, which again reveal he knows this Setting well.*] Wrapped in a blanket, [*He's outside versus inside a tent.*] he smiled up [*Clear emotional response.*] at the stars that extended from horizon to horizon. He breathed in the scents: the night orchids that hid their beauty shyly during the day and blossomed under moonlight, the release sourness plants, and the sudden love vegetables. [*Specific details.*] He listened to jungle music: the choir of birds and beasts that sang through the night. The air was so fresh [*Sensory details.*] he could feel his insides waking from a long polluted hibernation. [*Characterization.*]

NOTE: Showing the same Setting from two or more character's POVs can be an effective technique to let the reader in on conflict that one character may know about, but another doesn't.

Here's another example that gives the reader a strong sense that problems are just around the corner:

It's too bad really, that they hold the reaping in the square—one of the few places in District 12 that can be pleasant. The square's surrounded by shops, and on public market days, especially if there's good weather, it has a holiday feel to it. But today, despite the bright banners hanging on the buildings, there's an air of grimness. The camera crews, perched like buzzards on rooftops, only add to the effect.

—Suzanne Collins, *Hunger Games*

If you look at the passage above closely, there are not a lot of specific details—*square's surrounded by shops, bright banners hanging on the buildings.* This could describe any town with buildings around a central square location. If YA author Collins had only described these images, the passage would have fallen flat and not added to the conflict or emotion of the story. But by interspersing the vague images with stronger emotions that contrast with each other, the reader knows that something bad is just ahead.

Let's pull this last Setting description apart in greater depth to see why it is so effective.

> It's too bad really, [*Starting with the POV character's internalization, her thought process, sets up the contrast that's about to unfold.*] that they hold the reaping in the square—one of the few places in District 12 that can be pleasant. [*And here most readers have an image of a town square of sorts, though the details can vary a great deal from locale to locale. But the details are not what's important here. The fact that this place can be pleasant is what the reader is meant to focus on.*] The square's surrounded by shops, [*Now the reader has a stronger image of the space, but there's a world of difference between St. Peter's Square in Rome, Trafalgar Square in London, and Times Square in New York City. Collins doesn't want you to focus on the specifics—she is building a sense of a limited space, hemmed in further by buildings.*] and on public market days, especially if there's good weather, it has a holiday feel to it. [*Again, an emotional beat that's comfortable, okay, and reassuring.*] But today, [*Here's a transition phrase that alerts the reader that all is not as it seems. There is underlying tension beneath the bucolic space and this layers in the conflict subtext.*] despite the bright banners hanging on

the buildings, [*Another visual—we don't need to know the colors or images on these banners, or if they are of canvas, cotton, or silk. In another story those details might paint a richer Setting, but the author did not want that here. She wanted the focus on the contrast between what the POV character thinks about this place and what's about to happen. This is how she increases tension.*] there's an air of grimness. [*Specific word choices telling readers what she will show in the next sentence.*] The camera crews, perched like buzzards on rooftops, [*Powerful verb choice that creates a very specific image of foreboding and impending death.*] only add to the effect.

Collins shows that it's the contrast between the peacefulness of the town square and the following setting descriptions—*air of grimness, perched like buzzards*—that creates strong conflict on the page.

> **NOTE:** Not all telling should be eliminated from a writer's story. If you are telling only—*she felt frustrated, he was angry*—this can create weak writing, However, telling and then showing, or showing and then telling at times can help clarify for the reader what you want them to experience at a key point in the story.

What's important to remember about conflict in Setting is that it's a subtle but effective way to add strong emotion, such as foreboding, to a scene. Do all writers use it? No, but it's rare to find a *New York Times* bestselling author who does not.

What Not to Do

- Don't forget that conflict raises story questions, which keeps a reader turning pages.
- Don't use only dialogue or misconception as the only source of conflict.
- Remember that conflict can not come out of the blue for the reader. Doing so can pull them out of a story.
- Try not to use only external conflict or only internal conflict throughout a story. A good story needs both.

- Don't use a consistent repetitive pattern of descriptive word choices every time you describe a Setting—the *big, dark* house on the *tall, wooded* hill next to the *small, quirky* town.
- Don't use telling only when you can tell and show, or show alone.
- Never assume your reader understands your story conflict if revealed only once in your story.
- Don't forget that conflict can be built in layers throughout your story.

Assignment

Part 1

Use the following writing prompt about two different characters and craft a short passage showing how the Setting creates conflict for one character or the other.

Tyler is a street thief who has survived on his own in Los Angeles for several years. But this evening a gang member corners him in a dead-end street. Describe the Setting from Tyler's POV and then write it again from the gang member's POV. Can you show how what acts as conflict for Tyler might be seen as an asset for the gang member? Or what does Tyler see around him that he can use to his advantage? Does the gang member see that element of the Setting in the same light?

OR: Brandi is entering a new school environment—her seventh school since the beginning of the school year, and it's only January. Brandi doesn't expect to be at this school long, but she also knows that as the new kid, every day can be filled with landmines. Write a short, one-paragraph passage showing the school Setting, inside or out, and how what Brandi sees reinforces her sense of impending trouble.

Part 2

Look at your own WIP. Find a Setting that's currently devoid of conflict or could be enhanced by using some conflict.

A Writer's Guide to Active Setting

Can you focus in and see any ways to ratchet up the conflict or complications as compared to what you have on the page currently?

Look to thread specific word choices, action verbs, and details through what you currently have without adding too many words to the passage.

Recap

- Use a character's positive or negative response to a place to show potential conflict in the story.
- Contrast what the POV character is used to, or knows well, with a new environment in order to show a potential point of conflict.
- Bracket positive Setting words with negative ones to focus on a negative feel of a place, or negative words bracketed by positive to give a positive feel.
- Combine conflict and emotion in a Setting description for a stronger one-two punch on the page.

06

Using Setting to Show Backstory

Defining Backstory

What is backstory? *The Free Dictionary by Farlex* uses this definition: "The experiences of a character or the circumstances of an event that occur before the action or narrative of a literary, cinematic, or dramatic work."

Simply, backstory is anything that has happened before your current story that impacts what will happen in your story. Let's say your character likes to eat beets. Yes, that's a decision made before your story begins, but if it doesn't impact your story, it isn't a necessary part of the backstory. Your character losing her mother and father in a fatal car accident and thus avoiding vehicles whenever possible, even when she must save the world—that's backstory.

Newer and even some more experienced writers struggle with how to filter in backstory. Very new writers tend to dump a lot of backstory in the first few chapters—telling the reader that "x" has happened to this character, which is why they are broken, disillusioned, or afraid now. That's called an information dump and nothing is more effective in stopping the forward momentum of a story than throwing a lot of past history at the reader.

Why? What's happened in the past is over and done with. Not a lot of story questions are raised by past events. For example, look at the difference between these two sentences:

PRESENT: A car races toward her.

A story question—what's going to happen—is raised and keeps the reader turning pages to find out what's going to happen next.

PAST: A car had raced toward her when she was seven.

Since she's in the current story, we know she survived, so the story becomes diluted. We might be curious as to how she survived, but we also know she's somewhat okay, so the story question does not create as much tension on the page as what's happening now.

NOTE: Backstory matters only if it is relevant to the current story choices, decisions, or events.

In this initial example, the POV character has arrived at the home of a murder victim's spouse; he is examining her house as he prepares to tell her that her husband has been killed. This is not the kind of passage most writers would think to maximize in order to reveal some character backstory. But let's look at how Lee Child uses his first glimpse of the home to slide in a hint of his character's backstory. Notice how he uses contrast between what the character is seeing and what he's thinking.

> A watery sun was shining on it. There was a faint breeze and the smell of woodsmoke in the air and a kind of intense cold-afternoon quiet all around us. It was the kind of place you would have wanted your grandparents to live … It reminded me of the places in the picture books they gave me in Manilla and Guam.
> —Lee Child, *The Enemy*

> A watery sun was shining on it. [*Start of a build-up with sensory details, but not too much yet.*] There was a faint breeze [*Tactile.*] and the smell of woodsmoke in the air [*Scent.*] and a kind of intense

cold-afternoon quiet all around us. It was the kind of place you would have wanted your grandparents to live … [*Small steps to the image of a perfect home and the sense of family and belonging—then the punch line revealing backstory.*] It reminded me of the places in the picture books they gave me in Manilla and Guam.

Sums up a lot in a brief paragraph. What if the author hadn't taken the time to really dig in here and maximize the Setting? He might have written:

ROUGH DRAFT: I had been a child who had grown up on military bases around the world, who had never had what I saw as a traditional American home.

This version has emotion but it tells, not shows, and showing creates the richness—the worldbuilding that's intentionally used by the best authors via their attention to Setting details.

Using Contrast

Using Setting to reveal backstory in snippets not only keeps the reader anchored in the current story but also reveals much about the character in small, digestible, but powerful nuggets.

Consider if the POV characters are familiar with this location, if the Setting reminds them of something familiar, if the Setting lets the reader know how far they've come in the world, or how out of their element they feel. All of this can be used to reveal backstory, as we shall see.

Let's dig in and see how some authors use Setting as a powerful tool to show backstory via contrast.

But every town had been promising. Every place at first had said, Here you go—You can live here. You can rest here. You can fit. The enormous skies of the Southwest, the shadows that fell over the desert mountains, the innumerable cacti—red-tipped or yellow-blossomed, or flat-headed—all this had lightened him when he first moved to Tucson, taking hikes by himself, then with others from the university. Perhaps Tucson had been his favorite, had he been forced to choose—the stark difference between the open dustiness there and the ragged coastline here.

—Elizabeth Strout, *Olive Kitteridge*

Strout could simply have told the reader:

INITIAL DRAFT: Kevin felt isolated and lost growing up. He went to the University of Tucson and liked it for a while but then moved on.

How boring is that? Strout wanted to bring the reader deeper into Kevin's personality by showing a bit of backstory. She focuses the reader on one place, and shows us very specific memories of that place and his emotional response to it, then contrasts it with where he is now.

Because of this powerful Setting paragraph, the reader can see that the POV character tried to find security and happiness but failed. The reader gets pulled into his emotions, his longings through the viewfinder of how he saw Tucson. The reader can relate to the universal experience of traveling to a new place to start over. Now we're rooting for him to find what he experienced for a short time, under the enormous skies of the southwest.

In this next example, the POV character is an MI-5 agent, and is recovering in a private hospital, badly wounded after a mission gone horribly wrong. Worse, this agent starts to remember something about the tragic murder of her parents when she was a small child and the only witness. She'd repressed the memories for years but now they are seeping back, including the first Christmas she'd spent with her grandfather, her only remaining relative, after the murder.

The damp odor of logs, newly stacked beside the fireplace, mixed with the smell that the Christmas tree spread through the Great Hall. Mulled cider simmered in a copper pot on the kitchen stove.

> Each time the cook and her helpers rushed by they left the smell of
> apples, oranges, and cinnamon in their wake.
> —Maureen Tan, *AKA Jane*

This is a lovely scene, almost the picture-perfect image of a Victorian Christmas. The Setting details of a Great Hall, logs waiting for the fire, and the scents of mulled cider contrast with the current location of the agent—a cold and sterile hospital room, remembering her past in small snatches, in pain and wanting to forget more than remember.

The author chooses to reveal a positive memory, something that should be a welcomed thought, but it only serves to remind the agent of everything and everyone she's lost. Two sentences are all it takes to paint a bit of backstory to contrast with the current situation.

Let's look at another example. Barbara Kingsolver shows the reader Alice's telescopic view of her world by what she focuses on in her surroundings. The middle-aged woman is at a point of change in her life—she feels discontent in her relationship with her husband, Harland, and feels trapped in a place that no longer nurtures her. Look how well Kingsolver shows rather than tells this:

> The sky is perfect black. A leftover smile of moon hides in the bottom branches of the sugar maple, teasing her to smile back. The air isn't any cooler outside the house, but being outdoors in her sheer nightgown arouses Alice with the possibility of freedom. She leans back in a porch swing, missing the squeak of its chains that once sang her baby to sleep, but which have been oppressed into silence now by Harland's WD-40.
> —Barbara Kingsolver, *Pigs in Heaven*

We want to root for this woman who wants to smile back but cannot as she sees herself snared in her current Setting and situation. We know she's a mother and that she once was comfortable here; she assumed she always would be but things have changed. This one paragraph of backstory via Setting description helps start off this character's story journey. What if Kingsolver had not taken the time to use detail the way she did?

FIRST DRAFT: Alice went outside to sit on the porch swing, where she thought of her dissatisfaction with her husband, Harland.

Pretty bland isn't it? We as readers do not get to see Alice or what's brought her to this point in her life. We just see an unhappily married woman.

So let's see if we can slide a little more backstory, through Setting, in here.

SECOND DRAFT: Alice leans back in a porch swing, remembering how it used to squeak when she rocked her baby to sleep. But Harland didn't like the squeak and oiled it so it was now silent.

A little more detail shares a lot more about Alice. As readers, we now start to empathize with her. Kingsolver taps into a universal experience, the act of looking back on something that might not have been great, such as a squeaky swing, and remembering with longing a time that contained what the present is missing. Now let's revisit one more time to see why Kingsolver's final draft works so well. She does not race through this small moment but builds on it to show and tell:

The sky is perfect black. A leftover smile of moon hides in the bottom branches of the sugar maple, teasing her to smile back. The air isn't any cooler outside the house, but being outdoors in her sheer nightgown arouses Alice with the possibility of freedom. She leans back in a porch swing, missing the squeak of its chains that once sang her baby to sleep, but which have been oppressed into silence now by Harland's WD-40.

—Barbara Kingsolver, *Pigs in Heaven*

Are you drawn deeper into the character's POV by reading what she notices of her Setting and how it impacts her? Can you see how it stirs positive memories of her past and contrasts them with her current feelings of dissatisfaction?

Here's another quick example, two sentences long, that helps sum up the childhood of a character in Nevada Barr's thriller. The author doesn't tell the reader that the girl lived in deplorable conditions with a mom who doesn't care about anything, including her; instead she shows it when a teenage girl arrives home.

> The kitchen was a mess of dirty dishes. A Miller's can lay on its side weeping beer onto the linoleum, but the lamps were still upright and none of the dishes looked broken.
>
> —Nevada Barr, *13½*

Notice in particular that the author does not stop with the telling phrase—*the kitchen was a mess of dirty dishes.* She tells and then shows. We're seeing this Setting through the eyes and experience of a teenage girl and, for some writers, the telling portion would be enough. Then the reader would create his own image of a sink of dirty dishes. That could mean breakfast dishes with dried oatmeal or cold cereal on them, the popcorn bowl used the previous evening, or the used baby bottles waiting to be sterilized. But that's not the image Barr wants the reader to remember when thinking about this girl's early years. Barr makes sure the reader is in no doubt what's meant by adding the second sentence—*A Miller's can lay on its side weeping beer onto the linoleum, but the lamps were still upright and none of the dishes looked broken.* The very fact that the girl is thinking this is an improvement—that lamps knocked over and broken dishes are what she expected to see—reveals so much more.

And here's one more example where backstory is revealed by contrast with the current story. It's from my urban fantasy novel where the POV character has journeyed with two others to the Underworld. Since it's safe to say the average reader has never been to the Underworld, it was a little challenging to combine a Setting description along with revealing backstory from a POV character. The POV character, Kelly, with her companion, Mandy, has just left an area that was very uncomfortable and has arrived at a new location, brought by a woman who is neither friend nor foe at this point.

> It should have been an improvement but what Kelly saw behind the woman wasn't.
>
> A stone pathway replaced the slick mud path she and Mandy stood on. White sandstone, or maybe marble of a great age, created slanting walls on either side of the path, stepping back in space through a series of metallic wrought arches. Ornate, complicated arches ending in a gateway wide enough to allow entry for one person at a time.
>
> It sure wasn't like the gate to Kelly's backyard in Dubuque.
> —Mary Buckham, *Invisible Journey*

What I did here was set up that the POV character was seeing something that made her uncomfortable. There's a hint of emotion told to the reader. Then the Setting is described in three sentences with specific details making it clear there's an entrance way or gate in front of the character. The backstory is slipped into the last sentence where the character compares what she's seeing to what she knows from her background.

The reader doesn't need to have a description of Kelly's hometown gate spelled out since most of us have an idea of what a backyard gate in an Iowa town might look like. The intention of the short passage is to make it clear that Kelly is feeling out of her element by creating a specific Setting image and contrasting it to Kelly's comfort zone, which comes from her backstory.

NOTE: Don't be afraid of combining telling with showing to create contrast via Setting. It's using only telling that can trip up a writer.

Tying It All Together

Now let's look at some examples that not only use Setting to reveal backstory, but also employ a variety of the techniques we've explored in this book.

NOTE: The most powerful Setting can be used easily to show multiple techniques; for example, combining characterization, emotion, and backstory. Or backstory and conflict. You do not need to limit yourself to one technique per Setting description.

The following example comes from a story of a man on a downward spiral after an unexpected divorce. The author shows the ex-wife, Jen, looking at the new abode of the POV character. Look how much backstory you get about this couple, as well as conflict and emotions in one paragraph of Setting description:

> Jen looks pointedly at the crappy house in which I now live below street level. It looks like a house drawn by a child: a triangle perched on a square, with sloppily staggered lines for bricks, a lone casement window, and a front door. It's flanked by houses of equal decrepitude on either side, nothing at all like the small, handsome colonial we bought together with my life's savings and where Jen still lives rent-free, sleeping with another man in the bed that used to be mine.
> —Jonathan Tropper, *This is Where I Leave You*

Let's pull apart the example above to see not only how Tropper uses Setting to reveal backstory, but also to do just about every other thing we've studied in this book. This is why this Setting passage works on so many levels:

> Jen looks pointedly at the crappy house in which I now live below street level. [*Internalization by the POV character regard-*

ing what a secondary character is doing with clear negative word choices: crappy, below street level. *The use of the detail—below street level—creates a metaphor for the feelings experienced by the first-person POV character. The sentence also foreshadows the conflict between these two characters and what Jen, a secondary character, is about to see.*] It looks like a house drawn by a child: a triangle perched on a square, with sloppily staggered lines for bricks, a lone casement window, and a front door. *[Powerful word choices here build on what could be a charming description of a house—drawn by a child. But instead of charming, conflict is shown—a triangle perched on a square—followed by specific negative word choices:* sloppily staggered, lone window.] It's flanked by houses of equal decrepitude [*To make it clear the POV character is not in the lone lower-class house, but in an area of them, a much stronger statement.*] on either side, nothing at all like the small, handsome colonial [*Contrast using backstory via a description of their previous home with the current house.*] we bought together [*Backstory description showing how they were once a couple.*] with my life's savings [*Backstory revealing to the reader why the POV character might have grounds for his anger.*] and where Jen still lives rent-free, sleeping with another man in the bed that used to be mine. [*A powerful and subtle emotional punch. Tropper might have said Jen still lives in their old home with her new husband, but he doesn't. Instead he chooses a specific Setting in that house that sums up all of the POV character's bitterness and hurt.*]

Placing Backstory Setting Deep in a Scene

Here's another example. It's more than halfway through the story. Look closely at how the author takes a small visual of the seventeen-year-old boy POV character's room and shows the reader a lot about his past and present.

I wonder if other people use their bedrooms the same way I do. When things get packed full—like they are now for me—I retreat here. Since I was very young, Mom and I had an agreement that my room is private as long as I don't leave anything organic here long enough to change from a solid to a liquid giving off gases. If my clothes are within ten feet of the washing machine on wash day, they get washed. If not, they don't unless I wash them myself. That keeps her out of my room without an invite. I can't think of a time when I would have kept her out, but her respect for my private space has allowed me a true sanctuary. Which is what I need right now.

—Chris Crutcher, *Staying Fat for Sarah Byrnes*

What if the author wrote the standard:

My room was cluttered with clothes, some washed, some unwashed, with a poster of Michael Jordan on one wall and Superman on the other. My bed was plain and buried beneath last week's homework. The walls were pale blue, and a bulletin board hung over the desk.

See? It's a room, but all the reader sees is the room. He doesn't get any backstory on the room's occupant, a sense of emotion, conflict, or anything. It's just a room, so the forward momentum of the story is stopped, and would be held up even more if the description went on for a few more sentences.

Let's examine the Crutcher example one more time and pull out the micro-parts that make this simple description work harder.

I wonder if other people use their bedrooms the same way I do. [*Starts you in the mindset of the seventeen-year-old who's working at finding his place.*] When things get packed full—like they are now for me—I retreat here. [*Explains the internal motivation for how he uses his room. It's clear by his word choices that the room is a place of sanctuary*—retreat, when things get packed full, *needing to hide from things. It also adds conflict, raising a story question about what is happening in his world that he needs to hide from.*]

A Writer's Guide to Active Setting

Since I was very young, Mom and I had an agreement that my room is private as long as I don't leave anything organic here long enough to change from a solid to a liquid giving off gases. [*Shows backstory in the relationship between him and his single mother, as well as creates a fresh image of a room that any mother of a messy child—especially a teenager—can relate to.*] If my clothes are within ten feet of the washing machine on wash day, they get washed. If not, they don't unless I wash them myself. That keeps her out of my room without an invite. I can't think of a time when I would have kept her out, but her respect for my private space has allowed me a true sanctuary. [*More relationship disclosure between him and his mother, which is part of his backstory. Specific and consistent word choices—sanctuary, respect, private—that also shows us the emotional tenor of the relationship between mother and son as well as his loving, warm feelings toward her.*] Which is what I need right now. [*And the reader is shifted away from the room and back to the external action of the story. This also raises a story question, revealing conflict, about why he needs sanctuary.*]

Let's look at another example of a young man's room. The POV character is a housecleaner who uses her job as a means to keep distance between her and others, but she is very much aware of other people by observing how they keep their private spaces. Here, author Charlaine Harris shows the relationship between Bobo, a young man, and the housecleaner. She also threads in a bit of their backstory and shows the reader a little about him—a recurring character in the story series.

I stood in the doorway of Bobo Winthrop's room and eyed it grimly. Bobo is a husky seventeen-year-old, full of hormones in overdrive, as I'd discovered last summer. He was at school today. But his room was evidence that Bobo had been home to at least sleep and change clothes often during the past week. There was furniture in the room, somewhere, under all that mess, and I remembered it was good furniture, just as Bobo, I had a gut feeling, was a good kid—under all that mess.

In other words, he didn't leave his room like this to spite me after I thumped him in the guts for putting his hand on my bottom. It's just that Bobo has been accustomed all his life to having someone clean up after him.

Days like this, I feel like I'm following an elephant in a parade, armed only with a puppy's pooper-scooper.

—Charlaine Harris, *Shakespeare's Landlord*

Did it matter to the reader about the size of the room? The color scheme? The quantity or placement of the furniture? Not at all. The reader gets a sense of the personality of Bobo from his room, the relationship between the two people, and some backstory about both of them. Plus the passage foreshadows ongoing conflict for the housecleaner—*following an elephant in a parade, armed with only a puppy's pooper-scooper*—and adds in her emotional state of mind. Let's see what happens if we remove the Setting from the above passage.

> **ROUGH DRAFT:** Bobo is a husky seventeen-year-old, full of hormones in overdrive, as I'd discovered last summer. I thumped him in the guts for putting his hand on my bottom.
>
> He was at school today. I had a gut feeling Bobo was a good kid—under all that mess.

Takes a lot away, doesn't it?

Use Backstory Contrast to Raise Tension

Check out how, in the next example, Nancy Pickard manages to pull the reader deeply into the world and reveal the conflict of the story—a mystery involving events that happened between the POV character's husband and a fellow student while all three were in high school. The POV character loved school and excelled at it. Her police-captain husband was one of the wild boys in that particular environment, and his experiences there were very different than hers. The son he did not know he had is a current student at this school and has just showed up on the POV character's doorstep. This backstory is revealed to the readers before they get too far into the novel.

Much of the mystery element involves looking at what happened in this specific place, and what is still happening as a result of those key years. This approach slows the story and allows the reader to experience the school environment in a vivid way, through the first-person narrative POV. This includes some of the backstory of the school, which then pays off through the rest of the story. The theme of the novel, *Confession*, is understanding that one person's past is not the same as another's, yet that past can still define the present. Here the POV character starts to relate to the boy by understanding that not all her school memories were fun and exciting.

This passage, because of its length, slows the pacing of Pickard's novel, but because so much of the story is woven through what happened years ago in this school, Pickard takes the time to use the school Setting to foreshadow first from the wife, then from the husband—two very different school experiences. This backstory helps create conflict in the current story events.

> I had a sudden, startling memory of what it had been like to sit in those classrooms in late August, early September. Boys with their legs sprawled wide under their desks, their elbows taking up most of the aisle space. Girls with their chins in their hands, their other hands holding pencils, doodling on the cover of the steno pads they used to take classroom notes. All of us drooping, barely awake, now and then exchanging glances, arching our eyebrows at each other as the teacher droned at the front of the room. White chalk words on the chalkboard up front. All the windows open, but nothing moving in the stifling air inside where we were. A smell of bubblegum as somebody surreptitiously unwrapped a piece. The feeling of a scar in the wood of my desk, under my fingertips. The sense of the presence of the cute boy one row back to my left. The sweat at all the places on

> my body where my clothes were binding me. All of life on hold
> as if it were on hold waiting for the bell to ring.
> —Nancy Pickard, *Confession*

While the POV character might have personally liked school, she also remembers there were times when it felt stifling. This reveals a hint of backstory and conflict between the good and negative memories of this place. The reader gets a stronger sense of the emotional state of the POV character shifting from one emotional state—neutral memories—to stronger emotions—a life on hold, waiting for the bell to ring.

> **NOTE:** Weigh your usage of narrative Setting description against your intention. The longer or more narrative description you use, the slower your pacing.

Revealing More with Setting Backstory

Here's an example of Setting used to show the reader about the backstory and conflicted relationship between a son and his father: a father who recently died, leaving the son to deal with unresolved issues between them.

> Dad was obsessive about maintaining the house. He was a handy guy, always painting and staining, cleaning out the gutters, changing out pipes, power-washing the patio. He was an electrician by trade, but he gave it up to go into business, and he missed working with his hands, couldn't face the weekend without the prospect of manual labor. But now the paint is cracked and flaking off the window frames, there's an ugly brown water stain just below the roofline, the bluestones on the front walk rattle like loose teeth, and the rose trellises lean away from the house like they're trying to escape. The lawn hasn't been watered enough, and it's brown in patches, but the twin dogwoods we used to climb are in full bloom, their crimson leaves fanned out like an awning over the front walk. Consumed with Dad's slow death, Mom forgot to cancel the pool service, so the swimming pool in the yard glistens with blue water, but the grass is starting to come up through

the paving stones around it. The house is like a woman you find attractive at a distance. The closer you get, the more you wonder what you were thinking.

—Jonathan Tropper, *This Is Where I Leave You*

Do you get a sense of the father-son relationship here by what the son remembers about his father's behavior and the father's own conflicted choices? And a sense of how the father's slow, lingering death impacted his wife, too? This is accomplished through showing the deterioration of the family home while the mom's focus was getting her husband through his last months.

This is a strong example of using theme—the appearance of things versus what's really going on inside—to help the reader understand the emotional tenor of the story. This was not a sudden death, but a long, lingering one. The son had not made his peace with his father and is only now coming to terms with that issue. The Setting description thus reveals the emotional tone of the story, shows where the son is emotionally now, provides some backstory, and foreshadows conflict based on the realization that the POV character left his mother alone to deal with the dying process.

Next is an example of sharing backstory through showing the POV character's connection to a specific space. The author, Barbara Kingsolver, could have had the character simply respond verbally to the initial question and move along. She wanted to make a point that even though the POV character worked as a ranger in the nearby national park, she had chosen an isolated existence. As a result, her past belonged intimately to a nearby place, one she understands even if she doesn't choose to live there.

> "That your hometown?" he asked.
>
> She nodded, surprised he'd guessed it. They hadn't spoken for an hour or more as they'd climbed through the lacewinged afternoon toward this place, this view she now studied. There was a silver thread of Egg Creek; and there, where it came together like a

thumb and four fingers with Bitter, Goose, Walker, and Black, was
the town of Egg Fork, a loose arrangement of tiny squares that
looked from this distance like a box of mints tossed on the ground.
Her heart contained other perspectives on it, though: Oda Black's
store, where Eskimo Pies lay under brittle blankets of frost in the
cooler box; Little Brother's Hardware with its jar of free lollipops
on the dusty counter—a whole childhood in the palm of one valley.
Right now she could see a livestock truck crawling slowly up Highway 6, halfway between Nannie Rawley's orchard and the farm that
used to be hers, and her dad's. The house wasn't visible from here,
in any light, however she squinted.

—Barbara Kingsolver, *Prodigal Summer*

Look at the details Kingsolver uses to show the reader that the POV
character knows this town intimately—the name of each creek, the store
that sold a very specific item, a single vignette of the hardware store, the
name of a neighbor's farm, and the fact that her farm used to (past tense)
be there. Kingsolver has the POV character look at a specific Setting for
several reasons: to reveal the relationship of the character to the place,
to show her backstory, to anchor the reader into the emotional connection between memories and the character, and to give a clear sense of
a specific place.

What would have happened if Kingsolver had written a more prosaic description?

ROUGH DRAFT: Highway 6 ran from east to west through the
valley and passed her neighbor and her own former farmland. The
town was small with only one general grocery store and a small
hardware store. Five meandering creeks wandered across the
parceled farmland.

Do you get any sense of the place? Any sense of the relationship of the
POV character and that place? Any emotion? You probably don't feel a
lot. There's only a generic description, which is not active.

Now, lest you think that Setting must be delivered in larger paragraphs to show backstory, here's a quick, tight use in the opening of a chapter in a high fantasy novel.

> Only sometimes in the long evenings of July as she watched the western mountains, dry and lion-colored in the afterglow of sunset, she would think of a fire that had burned on a hearth, long ago, with the same clear yellow light. And with this came a memory of being held. …
>
> —Ursula K. Le Guin, *The Tombs of Atuan*

And here is a final example from a historical mystery series set in Louisiana in the mid-1920s. The protagonist, Dassas Cormier, has brought his young nephew to New Orleans for the boy's first visit. For readers of the series, they already know that Dassas left the New Orleans police force under a bit of a black cloud and returned to his childhood home, deep in coastal Louisiana near the Texas border. Pay attention to how the author threads in a hint of this backstory in this next passage. Rather than stopping the forward flow of the opening of this third book in the series, the author, S.H. Baker, uses Setting to reveal so much.

Look closely at how she combines sensory details, characterization, and backstory while transitioning the reader from the POV character being on a train coming to New Orleans, to arriving in the city. Remember that when you move a character from one Setting that's been described to a new Setting, make sure readers are not left with only a vague sense of the new place. Orient them quickly with a few details. If S.H. Baker had been less experienced as a writer, she might have written it this way:

> **FIRST DRAFT:** I stepped off the train into New Orleans. It felt like I'd never left it. I glanced at my nephew and waved him forward toward the boarding house I'd selected to stay in.

No sense of Setting here. No hint of backstory, no sensory details—nothing except an assumption that the reader already knows what New Orleans was like in the 1920s. Because of that erroneous assumption, later, when some detail of New Orleans is brought up—the heat, the station house, the steam trains—the reader can be jerked out of the story because that's not what she imagined while reading the earlier passage.

So how did S.H. Baker approach it?

> As soon as I stepped from the train onto the freshly swept platform, I had to smile. The city waited, as if nothing had changed since I'd left almost a year earlier. Heat carried scents of shellfish, jasmine and ladies' perfume, and hoards of people rushed to and fro from trains. Ahead, the massive brick station sprawled over a city block, and arched doorways beckoned like the arms of a woman. I took a deep breath, catching whiffs of freshly cut grass. Steam hissed from the trains behind me, momentarily overrunning voices raised in cheerful salutes and wailing farewells.
>
> —S.H. Baker, *Death of a Dancer*

Pulling it apart:

> As soon as I stepped from the train onto the freshly swept platform, [*Here is a quick telling of transition, but the author doesn't stop with "from train to platform." She added the small fact that it'd been swept, which creates a historical detail built on other historical details up to this point, and paints an image of a time when a clean platform was something noticeable.*] I had to smile. The city waited, as if nothing had changed since I'd left almost a year earlier. [*And here is where some backstory is threaded in. If left at this point, the reader would know he's been in New Orleans before but nothing more—was it for a few days or a few years? By continuing with more Setting information, the reader has a stronger sense of this man's connection to this place.*] Heat carried scents of shellfish, jasmine and ladies' perfume, [*And here are*

A Writer's Guide to Active Setting

*specific sensory details—texture (heat), plus smells, which allow
the reader to experience New Orleans more deeply.*] and hoards
of people rushed to and fro from trains. [*Here's some specific
action, plus the phrasing gives a historical flavor to the internal
observation.*] Ahead, the massive brick station [*Now we have
a clear visual of a historical building.*] sprawled [*Strong action
verb which paints a better image.*] over a city block, and arched
doorways beckoned like the arms of a woman. [*Fresh way of
describing archways and clearly coming from the POV of a young
man.*] I took a deep breath, catching whiffs of freshly cut grass.
[*Another sensory detail but one not often associated with a modern train station, so this builds in a little more historical detail.*]
Steam hissed from the trains behind me, [*Sounds and historical detail.*] momentarily overrunning voices raised in cheerful
salutes and wailing farewells.

Lots of information has been imparted to the reader in one short passage via Setting.

Next time you are using Setting in a story, consider if the POV
character is familiar with this location, if the location reminds him
of something familiar, if the location lets the character know how far
they've come in the world, or how out of their element they might feel.
All of these elements contribute to revealing backstory.

What Not to Do

Remember to keep your focus on the Setting to reveal the character.

> **YOU SHOULD DO THIS:** The root cellar reminded her of
> Gram's; the loamy scent, the cool, dark shadows, the shelf upon
> shelf of canned pears and cherries. Any moment Gram could holler
> down and ask for more onions or potatoes with dirt still clinging
> to their skin.

NOT THIS: I loved my grandmother's root cellar that was just like this one. She'd say "grab me some spuds," and I'd ignore the request as long as possible, until her voice would raise in pitch and urgency.

The first version shows the Setting. You are in the room with the character while learning more about her backstory at the same time. In the second version, the focus is only on the characters and a memory. You can use this in your work, but why use a passage that reveals only one thing—characterization in this case—when you can do double duty and show Setting as well as characterization, conflict, or emotion?

Assignment

Part 1

Think of your childhood home and your current home. Write a one-paragraph description that contrasts the two, while revealing some information about your past, what you valued. How does growing up in that place define you, or how does living in your current location define you in a way your childhood home never could?

Now take the childhood home of your protagonist and write a one-paragraph description that shows how that place created the person he or she is today.

Part 2

Find a Setting in your own WIP that's currently devoid of backstory, or could be enhanced with it.

Can you focus in and see any ways to bring up the POV character's backstory?

Consider adding a contrast between now and the past. Or use a memory of a specific Setting from the past with a Setting that you currently have on the page, without adding too many additional words to the passage.

Recap

- Backstory Setting can be contrasted with current story Setting for more power on the page.
- Use Setting to reveal information that has happened in the past to the character in small, digestible, but powerful nuggets.
- Combine backstory Setting information with other techniques of Setting—showing emotion, foreshadowing, reinforcing story theme, and adding conflict as opposed to adding only one technique at a time.
- Challenge yourself to use all of the techniques revealed in this book as you revise your manuscript. The more you stretch as a writer, the stronger your story becomes.

PART THREE

ANCHORING, ACTION, SETTING AS A CHARACTER,

MORE

Overview

In strong writing, there is always an overlap of craft techniques, resulting in a more integrated story. Nothing lives in isolation. So, for those who have read the first two sections in this book, you will notice that anchoring enhances what you learned about characterization in Part I, and Setting in an action sequence relates to elements of conflict in Part II. This is necessary both for combining the elements into a seamless unit and for helping you assimilate by repetition.

We will look at different concepts and examples in this next section, so you don't need to read the earlier sections to understand and embrace the concepts here, but these concepts build on one another as blocks laid in an interlaced pattern create a strong structure. The more you learn about writing Active Setting, the more you will be able to add depth and texture to your writing as you explore opportunities to use the material.

07

Using Setting to Anchor the Reader

Using Setting to anchor, or orient, the reader as to the *when* and *where* of the plot is very important to your story's success. Anchoring is created when the reader is better able to picture the *when* and *where* of the story, which creates a stronger emotional tie to the characters in the story, and thus to the work as a whole.

Since most of us have read only published novels, it's hard to show how this small detail can separate the published from the unpublished, but if you've had the chance to read unpublished work for contests, or worked with newer writers, you've likely seen this lack of anchoring time and time again. There's a reason for this lack—two, actually.

The first reason, and the most common one, occurs because writers can be so deep into the world of their characters that they assume more information is on the page than there really is. So when they say *mountain*, they assume the reader can see a ten-thousand-foot former volcano. But the reader may imagine a thousand-foot bump rising out of a flat landscape, or a jagged granite edifice that fronts more mountains, such as how the Rocky Mountains look traveling west from the plains. The reader's vision is based on her knowledge and experience, if what's shown on the page isn't clear.

If a character is flying a plane that has lost power in midair and is heading right for the mountain, these interpretations will make a huge difference.

> **NOTE:** Specific details can paint a much clearer and stronger image for the reader than generic, vague details. If the Setting matters to the story, aim for the specific, like making that plane heading for the mountain a Cessna 206 or a Boeing 747. Small details can paint very different images for the reader.

The second most common mistake is forgetting that the reader may have set the book down at the end of the last chapter, or scene, or you have ended a scene in one location and opened the next chapter, or scene, in a new location. Either way the reader needs to get re-oriented quickly so they can slip back into the story world and move forward with the action.

> **NOTE:** Always be aware of your intention on the page. The more detail or words allocated to a description, the more you are telling the reader that this Setting matters. If it doesn't matter, don't give weight to the Setting by being overly specific with the description of a room, a city block, or, as above, a mountain.

Using POV to Anchor Setting

Think about how you can anchor the reader in the Setting early in the scene. One way to do this is by actually describing the Setting in an omniscient way, with a big overview perspective. This means the scene is not seen or experienced through the POV of any of the characters, but instead is viewed as if the reader is looking through a camera lens that's been pulled back to give a panoramic sense of place. Look at the following example from Robert Ludlum's *The Icarus Agenda*:

> The angry waters of the Oman Gulf were a prelude to the storm racing down through the Strait of Hormuz into the Arabian Sea. It

was sundown, marked by the strident prayers nasally intoned by bearded muezzins in the minarets of the port city's mosques. The sky was darkening under the black thunderheads that swirled ominously across the lesser darkness of evening like roving behemoths. Blankets of heat lightning sporadically fired the eastern horizon over the Marran Mountains of Turbat, two hundred miles across the sea in Pakistan. To the north, beyond the borders of Afghanistan, a senseless, brutal war continued. To the west an even more senseless war raged, fought by children led to their deaths by the diseased madman in Iran intent on spreading his malignancy. And to the south was Lebanon, where men killed without compunction, each faction with religious fervor calling the other terrorists when all—without exception—indulged in barbaric terrorism.

—Robert Ludlum, *The Icarus Agenda*

Notice the description comes from far away—a background briefing, so to speak—and not from a character. Sometimes the use of this omniscient POV is actually one character's POV, coming after the fact, or as a summation. This approach to Setting is most often incorporated in the opening of a book, but is used less often in today's publishing climate. Why isn't it highly recommended now? Because of pacing issues and the loss of immediacy.

A large chunk of description slows the pacing dramatically and, if the description is not chock-full of conflict and emotion as Ludlum managed with specific word choices, what happens too often is distancing, a sense of the reader being pulled back from the story. This distancing creates less of a connection between a reader and what's happening on the page. The more this occurs, and the longer it occurs in a novel, the easier it is for the reader to set the book down and wander off to find something that engages her more.

Another point to remember if you decide to use the omniscient viewpoint to orient the reader, is that if you describe a place, make that place matter to the story. Look again at the Ludlum description. This is not just any Setting. This is a part of the world that's rife with conflict and darkness, something Ludlum conveys based on what he chooses to show his readers and how he's showing it.

Notice how he mixes "emotion" words—*sky was darkening, black thunderheads that swirled ominously, like roving behemoths. Blankets of heat lightning fired the eastern horizon*—and "specific physical anchoring" words—*over the Marran Mountains of Turbat, two hundred miles across the sea in Pakistan. To the north, beyond the borders of Afghanistan ... To the west ... in Iran, to the south was Lebanon ...*

Can you see as well as feel the locale? All that's needed is for a character to walk into this dark, threatening Setting and the reader is already rooting for his survival.

Let's look at another example, one not so dark:

> Amity Harbor, the island's only town, provided deep moorage for a fleet of purse seiners and one-man gill-netting boats. It was an eccentric, rainy, wind-beaten sea village, downtrodden and mildewed, the boards of the buildings bleached and weathered, their drainpipes rusted a dull orange.
> —David Guterson, *Snow Falling on Cedars*

Here the omniscient viewpoint gives a quick snapshot of the place while also indicating the emotional tone of the location. Words such as *wind beaten, downtrodden, bleached,* and *weathered* all paint a specific image of a certain type of depressed coastal town. The reader is quickly oriented into the *where* of the story, and is ready and waiting for the *who* of the story and what is about to happen.

If you choose to use omniscient POV, research whether this approach is used in the genre in which you're writing (for example, you see the technique more in the openings of historical novels, women's fiction, and literary fiction rather than romance and thrillers). Be sure to use omniscient POV with a light hand. Don't go on for pages and pages, because the longer you do, the slower your story will become and the greater the distance between story and reader. One last warning on using omniscient POV in your story before we move on. Omniscient POV is best used at the opening of a novel, or a scene, as opposed to pulling out of a character's POV to show an overview, then sliding back into the character's POV.

Otherwise you create a pattern of shifting POV that is disorienting for the reader and can actually create a physical sense of being yanked out of a story and then forced back in. Every time you shift POV, you risk losing the reader. Doing so, simply to show a Setting, is not worth the risk.

Let's now examine a quick one-line opening to a YA story that not only anchors the reader into the season of the story, but also into the mindset of the POV character. The author, Scott Westerfeld, doesn't have to shout that this is not a stuffy adult novel, he makes it very clear with this one killer opening line.

> The early summer sky was the color of cat vomit.
> —Scott Westerfeld, *Uglies*

What if the author had approached this fresh and fun opening line from a different direction? Like this:

> **FIRST DRAFT:** It was summer and I was missing my best friend so much, and my life sucked.

Okay, but nothing memorable and no visuals at all, simply an internal dialogue that sounds like it could be about any angst-ridden teen written by an adult. What if the author ignores the Setting and focuses more on what's seen from the POV of a fifteen-year-old girl, very unhappy at being the last of her peers to turn sixteen and waiting to have her whole world change.

Like this:

> **SECOND DRAFT:** It was early summer with the same pale-blue sky and the same yellow sun shining as it had for the last twenty-seven days.

A little more visual, though not fresh, but at least the Setting builds to the emotional sub-text that nothing was changing and the POV character was simply waiting for something. This could work for some novels and for enough readers that it might be published. But it doesn't create that eye-opening shazaam of Westerfeld's opening line that promised the reader—young adult or not—a story clearly told from the POV of a teen who is either looking at a very different world or sees her world very differently.

Use Deeper POV to Anchor Setting

Deeper POV means we are seeing something—in this case, Setting—through a character's eyes. Below is an example, from Barbara Kingsolver, of a Setting shown from deeper POV. The reader sees the Setting from the experience and emotions of one of the story's protagonists, which creates not only a stronger sense of place, but a stronger connection to the character, and thus to the story.

But before we dive into Kingsolver's amazing prose, let's imagine what could have happened if she had chosen to write without an eye to using Setting to its full advantage:

> **FIRST DRAFT:** Alice sat on her porch and thought about how unhappy she was.

Not much there. No Setting to give us a feel for this story, where it's happening or when. So let's try again:

> **SECOND DRAFT:** Alice sat on her Kentucky porch. She was very unhappy.

Now we have a general location but the rest is telling. Plus, there's a world of difference between a porch on a home in the Lexington horse country, and one on the Appalachian hill area, along the Ohio River, or in an urban Louisville neighborhood. So let's see how Kingsolver uses

Setting to bring the reader deep into the story from her character's POV, while also giving a strong sense of time of year.

> In the record heat of this particular Kentucky spring the peonies have blown open their globes a month ahead of Memorial Day. Their face-powder scent reminds her of old women she knew in childhood, and the graveyard. She stops swinging a minute to listen: a huffling sound is coming from the garden. Hester Biddle's pigs. Hester lives a short walk down the road and has taken up raising Vietnamese miniature potbellied pigs for a new lease on life after her stroke. She claims they're worth two thousand per pig, but Alice can't imagine on what market. They're ugly as sin and run away for a hobby, to root in Alice's peony beds.
> —Barbara Kingsolver, *Pigs in Heaven*

Kingsolver gives the reader a clear sense of season and place. But she also foreshadows a growing emotional disconnect between the character and where she was in her life by key phrases—*old women she knew in childhood, the graveyard, for a new lease on life*. Kingsolver uses these references from the POV character's impressions to show the reader the character feels herself aging.

We also experienced some fresh sensory details. Can you smell the flowers and hear the pigs? You are not only in a specific place at a specific time of year, but are experiencing that Setting from Alice's thoughts and worldview. It's much stronger than simply writing a few lines of description of this hardscrabble farm.

Here's another example where the author orients both the POV character and the reader, early in the story. This is from a mystery series by Nevada Barr that features a park ranger who moves from one national park to another, so the author not only wants to anchor new readers to the series, but also remind existing readers that this specific Setting is being seen for the first time by the protagonist as well.

Before we jump to this passage, though, let's again imagine that the author has a first draft version that needs some work. Something such as:

FIRST DRAFT: She was swimming in the waters off the Florida Keys.

Pretty ho-hum. As a reader we know where she is, but there's not much to engage us in such a way that, if we have never been to this part of the world, makes it memorable. She's simply in some water in some place.

SECOND DRAFT: She was swimming in the blue-green, warm waters off the Florida Keys, near enough to her new duty station to see Garden Key.

A little more orientation and thus anchoring. We might have a stronger sense of where in the Keys we are, even if we don't know the area, but we don't have a hint that this Setting matters to the story.

Barr's use of specific details in the opening of her story makes it clear to the reader that this Setting is a key part of her story world. With that information the reader can care about where the character is, as opposed to a generic ocean Setting that the character is soon going to leave. If you are not specific in how you've set up the world of your story, the reader can't experience it as you intended.

NOTE: If you are not intentional with the Setting specifics that you give your reader, they won't see what you see.

Let's observe how Nevada Barr anchors the reader at the opening of her story:

> The sky was as blue as the eye-watering fishes and every bit as merciless as the sea. The ocean was calm. Even with her chin barely above the surface she could see for miles. There was remarkably little to soothe the eye between the unrelenting glare of sea and sky. To the north was Garden Key, a scrap of sand no more than thirteen acres in total and, at its highest point, a few meters above sea level. Covering the key, two of its sides spilling out into the water, was the most bizarre duty station at which she had served.
> —Nevada Barr, *Flashback*

Let's examine her anchoring more closely:

> The sky was as blue as the eye-watering fishes and every bit as merciless as the sea. [*This line gives the reader a specific visual image, which also evokes a specific emotional feel given the word choices.*] The ocean was calm. Even with her chin barely above the surface she could see for miles. [*Now the reader has more visual images that will come into play later in the story when the character is trapped underwater in this same area. The reader will know it's isolated.*] There was remarkably little to soothe the eye between the unrelenting glare of sea and sky. To the north was Garden Key, a scrap of sand no more than thirteen acres in total and, at its highest point, a few meters above sea level. [*Here the author is very specific—and even if you don't know where Garden Key is on a map, you're starting to get a sense of this empty, flat Setting with a landmass that's not very large.*] Covering the key, two of its sides spilling out into the water, was the most bizarre duty station at which she had served. [*This last line reminds readers of the other locations in her mystery series without stopping the forward momentum of this current story. It also anchors the reader to where this character is now.*]

NOTE: Anchoring the reader when you are writing in deep POV means that Setting is seen through that character's interpretation and emotional state, her background, and her past and current experiences. It's not a generic, omniscient view from an all-knowing author.

What do you learn about the POV character and his world in the next passage? Is the character familiar with the location? How does the character feel about the location? About the world of the story?

> May in Ayemenem is a hot, brooding month. The days are long and humid. The river shrinks and black crows gorge on bright mangoes in still, dust green trees. Red bananas ripen. Jackfruits burst. Dissolute bluebottles hum vacuously in the fruity air.
> —Arundhati Roy, *The God of Small Things*

Pulling apart this short but powerful Setting description, let's pay particular attention to how the reader is anchored into the world of the character and his relationship to a specific place.

> May in Ayemenem [*Here we have a specific name of a specific place, but that's not enough by itself, unless this location is very well known to most readers. If this was London, Calcutta, or San Francisco, the reader might have some image of the Setting, but it may not be the image the author wants them to experience.*] is a hot, brooding month. [*Compound description here. The author did not stop with the word* hot, *but added a very specific emotional word to describe what the character feels about the heat.*] The days are long and humid. [*Now we're getting enough detail, including sensory detail, to feel the quality of the heat in this location.*] The river shrinks [*A visual most readers might not associate with heat, or associate only with a dry heat.*] and black crows gorge on bright mangoes [*Great, specific visual here: a power verb—*gorge—*combined with the black of crows against the brightness of mangoes spells out a more exotic spin on the location.*] in still, dust green trees. [*Nice contrast here so the reader sees the black birds gorging against not only green trees, which one would expect in a humid climate, but still trees, coated in dust. This is another sensory detail that can be felt, seen, and for some readers, even tasted.*] Red bananas ripen. Jackfruits burst. Dissolute bluebottles hum vacuously in the fruity air. [*And here three images create three beats. The first beat is ripening red bananas, not yellow. Second beat, the bursting of jackfruits. The average reader might not even know what a jackfruit is, but the powerful verb—*bursting— *helps create an image. Third beat are the flies, not just any flies but bluebottle flies, and are described as both dissolute and humming vacuously, all which leads to the last sensory detail: the scent of that humid, hot air—*fruity.]

There are enough specific, intentionally crafted details layered through this Setting description that, even if the reader has no idea where Ayemenem is, or if it really exists, they can experience it and are present with the POV character.

Now let's look at an example by author Meg Gardiner, who uses deeper POV and Setting to anchor the reader to the passage of time within the story. This information is threaded in at the beginning. Here the chapter opens with subtle clues to let the reader know *where* and *when* the new character is without stopping the action and forward momentum of the story. See if you can pick out the anchoring cues before we analyze this passage more closely:

> Later, Seth remembered cold air and red light streaking the western sky, music in his ears, and his own hard breathing. Later, he understood, and the understanding stuck in his memory like a thorn. He never heard them coming.
>
> The trail through Golden Gate Park was rutted and he was riding with his earbuds in, tunes cranked high. His guitar was in a backpack case slung around his shoulders. Crimson sunset strobed between the eucalyptus trees. When he reached Kennedy Drive, he jumped the curb, crossed the road, and aimed his bike into the shortcut through the woods. He was a quarter mile from home.
>
> —Meg Gardiner, *The Memory Collector*

Can you tell which city you're in by the name of that well-known park? Can you tell the time of day by the temperature and light—or a hint of the time before the author cues you into the exact time with a key word? Do you get a sense of where this individual is in relation to where he wants to go? Are there any sensory details that paint a stronger image?

Just a few key sentences, but the reader is there, in the skin of the character, Seth. The reader doesn't yet know how this event relates to other events that will be happening in San Francisco, but Gardiner uses Setting to anchor and orient the reader as to time and place. She also uses the contrast of place—Seth heading home—with something that happened to him. Let's pull apart this Setting for all the juicy insights it can teach us:

Later, Seth remembered cold air and red light streaking the western sky, music in his ears, and his own hard breathing. [*The reader is clear here that something is about to happen that will impact Seth, so it's important to know a hint of the build-up to what's currently happening to this person. We have sensory details here that indicate possible time of year and time of day—cold doesn't always happen in the winter; it could be a cooler summer, or late spring, or early fall when evening comes.*] Later, he understood, and the understanding stuck in his memory like a thorn. He never heard them coming.

The trail through Golden Gate Park [*Iconic name that sets the location as San Francisco. If the author said Central Park, or the Everglades, the reader would know which city or area of the country the story is set in. If the author used a generic name like Marshall or Liberty Park, the reader would have no idea where the story is unfolding.*] was rutted and he was riding with his earbuds in, tunes cranked high. [*More sensory detail.*] His guitar was in a backpack case slung around his shoulders. Crimson sunset [*One specific word—sunset—paired with a color visual to anchor the reader as to the time of day.*] strobed [*Action verb.*] between the eucalyptus trees. [*Specific foliage that again indicates California to those familiar with it. Even to those who are not familiar, you're not seeing cedar, or pine, or oak trees.*] When he reached Kennedy Drive, he jumped the curb, crossed the road, and aimed his bike into the shortcut through the woods. He was a quarter mile from home. [*By ending on this one word—a word that for most usually means security—the author uses Setting as a contrast to whatever has happened and raises a strong story question: Who stopped him from reaching home and where is he if he never made it?*]

NOTE: Weave Setting *whens* and *wheres* with dialogue or action details to keep from slowing the forward momentum of your story.

For another example, let's look at how mystery author Walter Mosley uses time-of-day changes to anchor the reader more deeply into his story. Mosley's Setting example is a hundred pages into his book, *Cinnamon*

Kiss, and at the opening of a new chapter. Note how the author uses deeper POV and Setting to quickly clue in the reader to the passage of time since the last chapter, explain where the POV character is, and give a hint of backstory through Setting—all of which gives readers a wonderful emotional check-in. Also note the use of sensory details. As if that's not enough, Mosley then ends on a clear contrast between the Setting and what the character is facing to remind the reader of the overall story goal. A lot is happening in one power-packed paragraph.

> I ate a very late lunch at a stand-up fried clam booth on Fisherman's Wharf. It was beautiful there. The smell of the ocean and the fish market reminded me of Galveston when I was a boy. At any other time in my life those few scraps of fried flour over chewy clam flesh would have been soothing. But I didn't want to feel good until I knew that Feather was going to be okay. She and Jesus were all that I had left.
>
> —Walter Mosley, *Cinnamon Kiss*

So now the reader knows it is late afternoon, receives some great sensory details of this specific San Francisco location, is a little deeper into where this character comes from, and then moves right back to the external issues driving the plot of this story.

Mosley creates a great emotional check-in by specifically choosing a remembered childhood Setting with a good emotional connotation and creating a contrast between what this character usually feels in the current Setting that creates that same connotation, and what he's feeling now. Since childhood memories are so strong, whatever situation he's in now must be really intense if it's overriding those memories. Another reason why using deep POV to describe Setting can be so effective.

Transitioning via Setting

Another place where you can maximize Setting to anchor the reader is when you transition the character or characters from one location to another. Sometimes using a scene break works best—the spacing on the page alerts the reader that the scene you were describing has shifted in POV, time, or location. But in some situations that approach can be too jarring. The secret is to transition the reader quickly, and not simply by dropping in sentences of plain description that don't work hard enough.

Look at how Robert Crais drops names of specific locations along with strong sensory detail to transition his POV characters from one location to another, and to show there's a passage of time during this period:

> … They climbed up through the Sepulveda Pass, then down the San Fernando Valley. The valley was always much hotter, and Pike could feel the increasing heat even with the air-conditioning. He watched the outside temperature rise on the dashboard thermometer. From Cheviot Hills to Van Nuys, they gained fifteen degrees.
> —Robert Crais, *The Watchman*

Look what happens if you remove the sensory detail of the heat in the above passage:

> They climbed up through the Sepulveda Pass, then down the San Fernando Valley. From Cheviot Hills to Van Nuys they traveled.

You no longer feel "in the skin" of the POV character and lose a large sense of where you are. Instead you're oriented simply by place names, which can work sometimes, but if they're used every time, a character shifting from place to place grows stale and redundant.

Another point to keep in mind is that it's not necessary to go in depth with the specific locations in your story every time you're approaching a transitional orientation. These transitions occur when you are quickly shifting the reader from one story Setting to another. What you're trying to do in a few tight sentences is give a strong sense of time and location passing.

If, instead of the greater Los Angeles area that Crais used above, we used locations in England, the passage might read:

> He drove south, catching the Clapham Road to avoid the jam of the A23, then down toward Croyden. The flat valley was always misty, and Pike could smell the tang of the salt air blowing off the Channel by the time he'd reached the M23 interchange. He watched the increase of seagulls and felt the decrease of temperature. From Pease Pottage to Brighton they lost seven degrees Celsius.

The reader might not know all these specific names or locations, but a few might seem familiar and she can get a strong sense of moving through a specific landscape over a period of time.

> **NOTE:** When an author is using Setting to transition the reader, the focus should be on moving from one place to another and not on the reader experiencing a particular Setting in great detail.

Here's another example, from the opening of *The Watchmen* by Crais, who is a master at using Setting in many powerful ways:

> City of Angels
> THE CITY was hers for a single hour, just the one magic hour, only hers. The morning of the accident, between three and four A.M. when the streets were empty and the angels watched, she flew west on Wilshire Boulevard at eighty miles per hour, never once slowing for the red lights along that stretch called the Miracle Mile, red after red, blowing through lights without even slowing; glittering blue streaks of mascara on her cheeks.
> —Robert Crais, *The Watchman*

In this example, Crais opens using Setting to anchor the reader while keeping the action high; the reader knows only that they are in the skin of a female. Some names help anchor us to a specific location—*City of Angels, Wilshire Boulevard, Miracle Mile*—but the focus is meant to be on the POV character versus the place. More of that will come later. For now the author wants a light brushstroke of Setting while keeping the focus on the character in action. In this particular example the author wants the reader to know the *where* and *when* of the story action through a secondary character's POV before transitioning to the protagonist's POV. In this story, Crais wants to show us this secondary character in action in a particular location before an accident happens that will change her life and the life of the protagonist. The reader needs to see this secondary character here before transitioning to the inciting incident (the event that sets off the chain of events that drive the story).

> **NOTE:** Transitioning happens when you need to shift the reader from one Setting to another, one POV to another, or one time to another.

What if Crais chose not to work so hard at his craft and removed the Setting entirely?

> THE CITY was hers for a single hour, just the one magic hour, only hers. The morning of the accident, between three and four A.M. when the streets were empty and the angels watched, she flew west on the Boulevard at eighty miles per hour, never once slowing for the red lights, red after red, blowing through lights without even slowing; glittering blue streaks of mascara on her cheeks.

It's still powerful writing but, with this opening, someone reading this for the first time will remain at a distance from the story, waiting for a stronger sense of where this story is happening. The *where* helps define the character in a concrete situation. A female blowing through Kansas City or Sequim, Washington, is a different character than one driving, as this character is, through Los Angeles. This example shows the character in her ordinary world (the world of the character before the story gets under way) and before she's transitioned into the events of the story.

In this next passage from a historical novel set in the 1920s, the reader enters the story in Paris, a city the POV character adores but was banished from for at least a year because of a scandal associated with her name. What this means is that the reader sees and experiences Paris for at least two or three chapters before we are transitioned to the exile destination—Africa.

Notice how the author begins with what the POV character knows well—city life—before transitioning to the uniqueness of this new Setting. Put yourself in the shoes of the POV character, banished for at least twelve months and sent to an environment that she knows nothing about. Now she sees it for the first time.

> The streets were paved and there were electric wires hanging overhead where colorful birds perched and monkeys swung hand over hand. There were plenty of motorcars, but the streets were choked with oxcarts as well, and rickshaws scuttled by, leaving the pushcarts to trundle in their wake, slogging through mule dung and rotting fruit. The air was pungent with both, and they combined with woodsmoke and the gum leaves and the sunburned red soil to give Africa its own unique perfume.
> —Deanna Raybourn, *A Spear of Summer Grass*

Let's pull this apart to see exactly how the author transitions the reader through this character's point of view.

> The streets were paved and there were electric wires hanging overhead [*Because most of the up-to-date European and American cities of the time had electricity, this would be familiar.*] where colorful birds perched and monkeys swung hand over hand. [*Here the author follows the familiar with the unique in detailing new Setting.*] There were plenty of motorcars, [*Back to what the character is familiar with.*] but the streets were choked with oxcarts as well, and rickshaws scuttled by, leaving the pushcarts to trundle in their wake, slogging through mule dung and rotting fruit. [*In this last sentence there were fewer words allocated to the familiar and more used to describe the new with both sensory details—*mule dung, rotting fruit. *There are also powerful action verbs—*choked, scuttled, trundle, slogging—

that all create a sense of urgency, movement, and life.] The air was pungent with both, and they combined with woodsmoke and the gum leaves and the sunburned red soil. [*And the last sentence of the paragraph focuses 100 percent on the new Setting, using sensory details of sight and smell, with specific details of woodsmoke (familiar), gum leaves (exotic), and red soil (combination of exotic to some readers, but familiar to others).*] to give Africa its own unique perfume. [*Then ends on the admission that what the character saw, smelled, and heard was different, but not necessarily negative. This raises a story question about whether the character will learn to appreciate this new Setting or hate every day she's not in Paris.*]

This author uses one paragraph of powerful Active Setting to transition the reader to a new location and makes sure the reader is there with the character.

Transitioning via Same Setting from a Different POV

The following is another example from Crais showing how he maximizes the Setting to pull a reader deeper into the same story, this time from a different character's POV. The reader knows the initial events happened in Los Angeles, but now we are transitioning to the protagonist's POV as he arrives at the scene of the accident.

First look at what Crais could have written in a rough draft, followed by what he did write, in order to see that enhancing the Setting might take a few tries, but it's well worth the effort:

> **ROUGH DRAFT:** They drove toward south LA to the more industrial area.

Does this tell the reader much? What visuals are you getting? We know the characters are in Los Angeles, but the word *industrial* could mean strip malls to one reader, factories to another, or a green solar or wind field to yet another.

REVISED ROUGH DRAFT: They drove south from Glendale into a dirtier, grittier, more industrial area of LA.

Now we have some stronger visuals—and sometimes this is all a story needs. There's just enough info to anchor the reader and let them know that since the characters are in this type of environment, they may not see small children riding plastic bikes on the sidewalk, or want to get out of their vehicle and have a picnic. But what if you want or need the Setting to show more, to really anchor the reader, or make a stronger point about the same story Setting experienced in a different way? Let's revisit how Crais uses Setting in the next paragraph:

> The drive south from Glendale was tedious with the heavy afternoon traffic, and ugly with the power cables and train yards that bordered the river. It was a dirty, gray part of Los Angeles that never seemed clean, even after the rains, and when they finally crossed back to the west side, the area in which Larkin lived wasn't much better. The streets were lined with warehouses waiting to be brought up to earthquake standards or razed, and other buildings housing storage units or sweatshops where minimum-wage immigrants built cabinetry and decorative metalwork. Everything about the area was industrial.
> —Robert Crais, *The Watchman*

Am I saying that every time you move your characters from one place in your story to another that you want to stop and place as much emphasis on detail? No. In this particular story the Setting plays a major role. It's the scene of a car accident that now has a wealthy heiress running for her life and Joe Pike and Elvis Cole—characters well known to Crais fans—trying to figure out what happened in order to save the girl.

Setting impacts different characters in different ways. Using Setting as you transition the reader to a different POV in the same place creates a stronger world for your story. This is a different approach than the one we will soon discuss in the section When Place Matters. Here the story could unfold in any large city. Los Angeles, as a specific Setting, is not core to the story, but the author wants to create stronger characterization to create subtext on the page.

Here's how Jamie Ford uses Setting and the movement of one of the main characters to really place the reader in a specific place (Seattle) and time (1942). Look at how the small, specific details work extra hard:

> As he walked along the damp sidewalks, his breath came out in a swirling mist, adding to the fog rolling in off the water. He tried to stay in the shadows, despite the fear that crept into his mind and curdled his stomach. Henry had never been out this late by himself. Though with the crowds of people that bustled up and down the avenues, he hardly felt alone.
>
> All the way down South King, the street was awash in the stain of neon signs that defied the blackout restrictions. Signs for bars and nightclubs reflected greens and reds in each puddle he jumped over. The occasional car would drive by, bathing the street in its dim blue headlights, illuminating the men and women, Chinese and Caucasian, enjoying the nightlife—despite the rationing.
>
> —Jamie Ford, *Hotel on the Corner of Bitter and Sweet*

Let's deconstruct these two paragraphs to better understand how Ford uses Setting to anchor the reader deep into the time frame and specific location of the story:

> As he walked along the damp sidewalks, [*Nice sensory detail, but by itself this could be any sidewalk in any city.*] his breath came out in a swirling mist, adding to the fog rolling in off the water. [*Now the reader knows there's a body of water nearby large enough to create the mist and damp.*] He tried to stay in the shadows, despite the fear that crept into his mind and curdled his stomach. Henry had never been out this late by himself. Though with the crowds of people that bustled up and down the avenues, he hardly felt alone. [*At this point we could be in a generic Setting except that we're deep into the story and know we're in Seattle. As a result, the sensory de-*

tails anchor us into this character's experience of this part of Seattle at this time of night.]

All the way down South King, [*Specific street name for those familiar with Seattle, placing the story near the area now called the International District.*] the street was awash in the stain of neon signs that defied the blackout restrictions. [*This key historical reference lets the reader know we're in World War II.*] Signs for bars and nightclubs reflected greens and reds in each puddle he jumped over. The occasional car would drive by, bathing the street in its dim blue headlights, [*Earlier in the story the reader was shown how car lights were muffled for the blackout so this reinforces that image.*] illuminating the men and women, Chinese and Caucasian, enjoying the nightlife—despite the rationing. [*Another reference to the time period.*]

Let's review the above passage for details that show the reader we're not in a contemporary world—*signs that defied the blackout restrictions; bathing the street in its dim blue headlights; despite the rationing.* If you visited this area of Seattle you'd experience a lot of the general Setting details—*damp sidewalks; fog rolling in off the water; South King; street was awash in the stain of neon signs.* Threading historical references and specific details of the Setting through ordinary details brings the reader deeper into the period of the story. The reader is transitioned by what they know firsthand—sidewalks, fog, a specific street name in Seattle— to what they have not experienced directly—blackout regulations, dimmed lights, and rationing.

Transitioning in Stories with Large Worldbuilding

Writers of fantasy, urban fantasy, sci-fi, steampunk, and paranormal often must introduce a whole new element of their world while keeping the forward momentum of the story line strong. Using Setting can help transition readers through a story, slowing the pacing to allow the reader to get a solid image of a new Setting, and then picking up the pace again as the story continues.

> **NOTE:** When first introduced into a new-world Setting in fantasy and SF stories, the reader is willing to slow down for the external events of the story just enough to be anchored into the new Setting. A few paragraphs or sentences are all that's needed. Not pages and pages of Setting details.

An example from an Ilona Andrews urban-fantasy series shows how she transitions the readers from one Setting of her story to a very different Setting. First, the reader is cued in to expect the Setting to change as the characters move from one realm to another:

> The California of the Broken was a desert in parts, she reflected. The California of the Weird was all mountains, lakes, and lush greenery.
> —Ilona Andrews, *Fate's Edge*

In this example, readers do not need to see specific lakes, types of trees, or shades of green. They only need to know they are moving out of one world—*the Broken*—into another—*the Weird*. The author starts with the normal details that the average reader is familiar with before transitioning to the specific details that show us how different the world of the Weird is:

> Far ahead on the mountaintop, cushioned with the foliage of the Weird's old forests, a castle thrust into the sky. Tall, majestic turrets and flanking towers of white stone covered by conical roofs of bright turquoise green stretched upward, connected by a textured curtain wall. ...
> "It's like a fairy tale," Audrey said.
> —Ilona Andrews, *Fate's Edge*

Let's dissect how Andrews transitions the reader from one unusual world into another:

Far ahead on the mountaintop, [*A known image to the average reader.*] cushioned with the foliage of the Weird's old forests, [*A detail that shows this Setting is different. Many readers might have heard of old-growth forests, but unless the reader lives in an area where they still exist, they are unusual and unknown.*] a castle [*Most readers get a visual of this from TV and movies.*] thrust into the sky. Tall, majestic turrets and flanking towers of white stone covered by conical roofs of bright turquoise green stretched upward, [*The details anchor the reader into this particular castle.*] connected by a textured curtain wall. [*And we're back to an unknown image. But because so much of the description is easily seen, it's okay—it does not throw us out of the story.*]

"It's like a fairy tale," Audrey said. [*Here the character says what the reader feels, which makes the visual real. Now we're transitioned to the world of the Weird.*]

NOTE: Once the reader has a general sense of the place and period of a story, it can be helpful to reinforce that information with key specific details throughout your novel. Setting is one way to do this.

Chapter and Scene Beginnings

In the opening of your novel, the reader is willing to give you enough word allocation to let him enter the world of the story, but only for so long before something must happen. He picked up your mystery, romance, fantasy, or general fiction novel to get lost in the world of your story. He could have picked up a *National Geographic* if he wanted a travelogue to read, so keep that in mind as you are using Setting in your opening.

Let's look how historical writer Susan Vreeland pulls the reader deep into the world of the west coast of Vancouver Island in 1906. Readers might not know what all the words mean or where the specific Setting, but they are given enough detail to see how this POV character sees her Setting:

Salmonberry, 1906

Letting her cape snap in the wind, Emily gripped her carpetbag and wicker food hamper, and hiked up the beach, feasting her eyes on Hitats'uu spread wide beneath fine-spun vapor. Cedars elbowing firs and swinging the branches pushed against the village from behind. One wayward fir had fallen and lay uprooted with its foliage battered by waves and tangled in kelp. Wind whipped up a froth of sword fern sprouting in its bark. At last, she was right here, where trees had some get-up-and-go to them, where the ocean was wetter than mere water, where forest and sea crashed against each other with the Nootka pressed between them.

—Susan Vreeland, *The Forest Lover*

Examining more closely, we can see how Vreeland anchors the reader deeply into the world of the story via Setting and sets up the relationship between the protagonist and her Setting. She also foreshadows the theme of the novel: one woman's love affair with the First Nations tribes and the coastal world of those tribes at the turn of the century:

Salmonberry, 1906 [*A device often found in historical, fantasy, science fiction, and thriller novels to clearly cue the reader into the where and when of the story.*]

Letting her cape snap in the wind, Emily gripped her carpetbag and wicker food hamper, [*Two small historical details that begin layering the time period. If she carried a backpack and thermos she'd clearly be in a later time period than 1906.*] and hiked up the beach, feasting her eyes on Hitats'uu [*At this point the reader has no reference to let them know what this word means, so the author makes sure it's clear in the next sentence.*] spread wide beneath fine-spun vapor. Cedars elbowing firs and swinging the branches pushed against the village [*Here we're informed Hitats'uu is a village.*] from behind. One wayward fir had fallen and lay uprooted with its foliage battered by waves and tangled in kelp. Wind whipped up a froth of sword fern sprouting in its bark. [*Look at the specific details she uses to paint this Setting versus the woods in South Georgia or Maine—cedars,*]

fir, kelp, sword fern not on the ground but growing along the bark.]
At last, she was right here, where trees had some get-up-and-go to
them, [*And here is the transition from just Setting to a clear sharing
of what this particular character feels about this Setting.*] where the
ocean was wetter than mere water, where forest and sea crashed
against each other with the Nootka [*Tribe name which will be expanded upon in the story.*] pressed between them.

This one paragraph of detailed description brings this forest environment, and the protagonist's relationship to it, alive. The next paragraph
contrasts where the POV character has lived prior to this time and how
she feels about those locations. In the final paragraph on that page the
author returns the reader to "west coast of Vancouver Island" so that
it's clearer where this Setting is.

The next example comes from the opening of book six in a mystery
series set in upstate New York, where the location is a vital element of
the story. What's important to note in this passage is how quickly and
seamlessly the author, Julia Spencer-Fleming, slides in enough Setting
details to anchor the reader on the first page. There's a lot of action going on, so the Setting can't stop the forward momentum and the pacing,
but without the Setting, the reader would be lost attempting to understand what's happening and where. There's also a nice contrast between
the bucolic Setting and what's happening.

When she saw the glint of the revolver barrel through the broken
glass in the window, Hadley Knox thought, I'm going to die for
sixteen bucks an hour. Sixteen bucks an hour, medical and dental.
She dove behind her squad car as the thing went off, a monstrous
thunderclap that rolled on and on across green gold fields of hay.

The bullet smacked into the maple tree she had parked under with a meaty thud, showering her with wet, raw splinters. She
could smell the stink of her own fear, a mixture of sweat trapped
beneath her uniform and the bitter edge of cordite floating across
the farmhouse yard.

A Writer's Guide to Active Setting

The man shooting at her turned away from the porch shaded window and yelled something to someone screaming inside. Hadley wrenched the cruiser door open, banging the edge into the tree. She grabbed the mic. "Dispatch, Harlene! This bastard's shooting at me!"

—Julia Spencer-Fleming, *I Shall Not Want*

Let's pull this opening apart to see how the Setting is made to work for the situation while not intruding on the action and tenseness of the passage.

When she saw the glint of the revolver barrel through the broken glass in the window, Hadley Knox thought, I'm going to die for sixteen bucks an hour. [*The passage opens with action: Her life's in danger and she's risking it for very little reward. The setting is a house with windows of broken glass and a weapon pointing at her, which ramps up the desperation of the situation. The emotion is in the internalization, but by layering in the Setting details, it's clearer the POV character is in a dangerous situation. If the house had been described as a split-level ranch or spit-and-polish townhouse, the tension would be decreased a little.*] Sixteen bucks an hour, medical and dental. [*Internalization.*] She dove behind her squad car as the thing went off, a monstrous thunderclap that rolled on and on across green gold fields of hay. [*Action and character information: She's law enforcement based on the vehicle. Setting: She's in the country, deep POV giving her personal association with what the sound means in contrast to the Setting. That detail of green gold fields of hay should have been a lovely image, but instead of hammering home the broken condition of the house, the author chose to contrast what should have been an idyllic landscape with what the character is dealing with. Plus the reader has a hint more understanding that this character might be isolated here, out in the country.*]

The bullet smacked into the maple tree she had parked under with a meaty thud, showering her with wet, raw splinters. [*Danger is rising: We know the shooter can reach her and her vehicle, which means he can shoot her if she tries to drive off. Senses: "Smacked with a meaty thud and showered wet splinters on her" pulls the reader deeper into the action via Setting, with a specific kind of tree for a stronger image.]* She could smell the stink of her own fear, a mixture of sweat trapped beneath her uniform and the bitter edge of cordite floating across the farmhouse yard. *[Nice emotional insight and a sensory detail that is added to the visual of a farmyard.]*

The man shooting at her turned away from the porch shaded window and yelled something to someone screaming inside. Hadley wrenched the cruiser door open, banging the edge into the tree. *[Action and a bit more Setting: We know she's trapped because she doesn't jump in the car and drive off.]* She grabbed the mic. "Dispatch, Harlene! This bastard's shooting at me!"

Now let's pull out all the Setting details that, if read alone, help anchor the reader just enough to where the character is—*broken glass in the window, green gold fields of hay, maple tree, farmhouse yard, porch shaded window, banging the edge* (of the car door) *into the tree.* See? Not a lot of information is needed to identify this character's location. Given the situation, too many details would detract from the life-and-death situation this character is handling. As the sixth book in the series, with the fifth one ending on a cliffhanger, this book does not open like some of the earlier novels, with more description of the Adirondacks in New York State. Instead it opens in action, which raises a lot of story questions that have the reader turning that first page to find out what happens next.

That's an important point to remember as you dig deeper into all the ways Setting can make a difference in your writing. Sometimes you want a light stroke, as Spencer-Fleming does above: just enough to let the reader know where the character is in space and if the Setting is hampering or helping the character achieve their scene goal. Other times you'll want to use the Setting to show the reader more—emotion, conflict, or backstory. When you use the Setting information to anchor a reader to where the events of the story are unfolding, always ask yourself how

A Writer's Guide to Active Setting

much the reader might need; don't overwhelm the reader with details you've shared already, or confuse them with too little.

> **NOTE:** Setting should always enhance your story, not detract from it. Be intentional when you use Setting. Be aware of why you are adding description and allocating more words.

Here's another opening from a different genre, a steampunk novel:

> Down in the laundry room with the bloody-wet floors and the ceiling-high stacks of sheets, wraps and blankets, Vinita Lynch was elbows-deep in a vat full of dirty pillowcases because she'd promised—she'd sworn on her mother's life—that she'd find a certain windup pocket watch belonging to Private Hugh Morton before the device was plunged into a tub of simmering soapy water and surely destroyed for good.
> —Cherie Priest, *Dreadnought*

The reader doesn't know the exact time frame yet, but there are a few clues—*windup pocket watch, tubs for washing, wraps among the sheets, and blankets.* What this author establishes with this particular Setting is anchoring the reader into the personality of the POV character, a woman who is willing to take on the work necessary to find a particular item belonging to a soldier. The next paragraph establishes that the character is in the laundry room of a hospital and doing the favor for a wounded soldier, and the story is off and running. The reader doesn't need to know a lot about the Robertson Hospital, or which war was happening before being introduced to the protagonist. We do get, in one paragraph showing the interaction of Setting and character, a sense of the world of the story.

> **NOTE:** Weigh how much the reader needs to know at this moment to see if you might be writing too much or not enough.

Since the most common place a reader is tempted to set down a novel is at the end of a chapter or scene, it's only logical that the author creates a quick and subtle anchoring for the reader at the beginning of the next chapter or scene.

Let's look at the following example from a novel by Janet Evanovich. The passage is the opening to chapter five, and the reader already knows she is in New Jersey, but Evanovich finds a subtle and humorous way to anchor the reader quickly into the specific *where* and *when* through the POV of the protagonist:

> Sitting in a coffeehouse leisurely sipping a latte wasn't on my morning schedule, so I opted for the McDonald's drive-through, where the breakfast menu listed French vanilla lattes and pancakes. They weren't Grandma-caliber pancakes, but they weren't bad, either, and they were easier to come by.
>
> The sky was overcast, threatening rain. No surprise there. Rain is de rigueur for Jersey in April. Steady, gray drizzle that encourages statewide bad hair and couch potato mentality. In school they used to teach us April showers bring May flowers. April showers also bring twelve-car pileups on the Jersey Turnpike and swollen, snot-clogged sinuses.
>
> —Janet Evanovich, *Seven Up*

We're clear that it's morning, and April, and Evanovich throws in some location-specific wry internalizations from the POV character to boot, using Setting to reveal character. No slowing of the action to flatly state, "It was the next morning and rain threatened."

Let's assume Evanovich had to build to this point:

FIRST DRAFT: It was going to rain in New Jersey.

The reader now knows he is in New Jersey, but since this particular novel is part of her popular Stephanie Plum series, which is set in New Jersey, it's pretty safe to say the reader already knew what state they were in by this point.

A Writer's Guide to Active Setting

SECOND DRAFT: I was having breakfast on a typical spring morning in New Jersey.

Not only is this an example of just telling, it assumes that the reader knows what a typical morning in the spring is like in this state. We're not anchored into this scene via the Setting. Look back at the passage again and determine how Evanovich quickly lets the reader know what time of morning it is, as well as how her specific character describes the time of year in New Jersey.

> **NOTE:** Orienting the reader at the opening of a new scene or chapter can be short and to the point. *Three hours later, the evening shadows slanted across the park. Fifteen minutes of brutal freeway traffic and I arrived.* The important element is knowing how much information the reader needs to know at this point in your story, and that depends on how you ended your last scene or chapter.

Chapter Opening Examples

Here are several chapter openings from Robert Crais. Notice how he quickly orients his readers and clues them in to the passage of time and change of location via Setting details, as he moves the readers deeper into his story:

> **CHAPTER 5**
> THIRTY-TWO HOURS earlier, on the morning it began, Ocean Avenue was lit with smoky gold light from the street lamps and apartment buildings that lined Santa Monica at the edge of the sea.
> —Robert Crais, *The Watchman*

Can you tell where you are, what time of day it is and get a hint of Setting that is specific to this place? Do you have an idea of the passage of time? Do you have enough images to anchor you quickly as to place?

CHAPTER 7

PIKE CRUISED east on Sunset Boulevard into the purpling sky, driving easy for the first time in twenty hours, invisible in the anonymous car. When they passed Echo Lake with its fountain, dim in the twilight, Pike turned north into the low hills of Echo Park. The houses would be nicer east of the park, but the twisting residential streets to the north were narrow and the homes were clapboard shotguns. Prewar street lamps were flickering on when they reached the address.

—Robert Crais, *The Watchman*

Again, the reader quickly knows the passage of time in this new chapter by what the POV character sees of the light. The character is not only driving through streets that keep the reader oriented, but also showing the passage of time via commenting on the change of lighting. Crais keeps the reader in the skin of the POV character by using the Setting effectively.

> **NOTE:** Using change of light is a quick-and-easy reference point to show the passage of time.

CHAPTER 8

The windows grew light by five-thirty the following morning, filling the Echo Park house with the brown gloom of a freshwater pond.

—Robert Crais, *The Watchman*

The previous chapter ends with the POV character in this house. A writer who doesn't know any better might jump to the character taking some sort of action the next morning or simply saying, "The next morning, Elvis Cole …" Crais sucks the reader right back to the *when* and *where* in one line before jumping to the POV character's actions. We are anchored more deeply into the story and see the day unfolding through Elvis Cole's POV filter. That's using Setting to the nth degree.

CHAPTER 18

IN THE QUIET of the later night, a violet glow from Dodger Stadium capped the ridges as Pike eased up to the Echo Park house.

> The air was warmer than the evening before, but the same five men still clustered at the car beneath the streetlight, and families still sat on their porches, listening to Vin Scully call a game that many of them knew nothing about only a few years before.
> —Robert Crais, *The Watchman*

The reader is deep into the story now but the author still doesn't neglect to orient the reader to the passage of time, use sensory details, and give the reader a hint of foreshadowing by referencing sights that were noted in a previous chapter.

> ### CHAPTER 19
> THE NEXT MORNING, Pike was cleaning his pistol at the dining table when the girl came out of her room. Pike had been up for three hours. It was ten minutes after eight.
> —Robert Crais, *The Watchman*

What if Crais had gotten lazy by this chapter? After all, it's halfway through the book. He could have written:

> **ROUGH DRAFT:** The next morning, Pike was cleaning his pistol at the dining-room table when the girl came out of her room.

What if he moved on with the story after this? The reader would have been confused: What did the author mean by "the next morning?" Was it nine, ten, or 11:56? By starting with a relatively vague description of time and deepening it by the end of the paragraph, the author paints a picture of Setting via time of day. And the reader better knows who these characters are based when they wake up and start moving about, as well as what they do first thing in the morning. We also receive a hint of unease here by focusing on how long Pike has been up, without stating this fact outright. This is the subtext of the passage.

Without slowing the story long enough to anchor the reader into the Setting, Crais would lose a chance to layer in clues and insights, potentially losing his reader.

Next-Day Scene Transitions

Here's another example, this one from a memoir, which transitions the reader from the end of the last scene when the writer went to bed. Here's how she started the next scene:

> Early the next day, when the stars still stitched the velvet sky and the rooster had yet to smooth his feathers, we made ready to leave.
> —Danielle A. Dahl, *Sirocco*

This debut author could have written a quick and easy line—*Early the next day we made ready to leave*—surmising that the reader would not put the book down between scenes, but she didn't. She dug deeper as a writer. By using two very specific, very clear indications that a new day had begun in war-torn Algeria, the reader is there, on scene, in that Setting.

> **NOTE:** As an author, don't assume that the reader should know the time of day, nor where the POV character is going. Give enough cues to anchor them, especially at chapter and scene changes.

What Not to Do

In the example below, all the reader knows is that the character has received a phone call telling him that a friend has been airlifted from an accident to an area hospital, and the character is on his way somewhere.

> "I'm on my way." Bill ended the call and pulled into Route 701's right lane, preparing to exit.

Any idea of where this character is? Do you know this is a hospital being referenced? What time of day? Season? Sense of urgency? This is the opening of the story and as long as the reader is trying to figure out the *where* and *when* of the story, he will remain slightly distant from the events of the story.

Let's see what we can do to anchor the reader more strongly into the Setting and the situation:

> "I'm on my way." Bill punched *end* on the phone and rocketed over into Route 701's right lane, ignoring the glare of the late afternoon March sun, as well as the four lanes of commuters streaming east out of Seattle toward Bellevue. What the hell happened to Steve to land him in an ICU unit?

With a few tweaks, the reader now has a better idea of where Bill is, the time of day, and a stronger sense of place, as well as of the emotion driving the scene.

Here is a bad example of a new story opening:

> He stood by my car, his skin buffalo-hide tough. Faded overalls, flannel shirt, dirty boots. A Yankee's baseball cap obscured his face except for his unshaven chin.

No idea what time of day it is, where these characters are, or how long since these two characters last saw one another.

Here's a rewritten example, designed to introduce the reader to the *when* and *where* of this chapter using Setting detail:

> He stood by my car, his skin buffalo-hide tough, the late-afternoon, New Mexico sun casting shadows across his face. Faded denim overalls, flannel shirt, dirty boots, his colors contrasted sharply with the subtle purples and dusty reds of the Sandia Mountains behind him. A John Deere baseball cap obscured his face except for his unshaven chin.

OR:

> Morning light bathed him as he stood by my car, his skin buffalo-hide tough. Faded denim overalls, flannel shirt, and dirty boots clashed with the white clapboard cottage to his left. A Red Sox baseball cap obscured his face except for his unshaven chin. Obviously he hadn't received the dress code for Martha's Vineyard.

Now it's your turn. Look at your WIP's opening, the opening of a chapter, or pick any scene that might need a little more work to help a reader understand the passage of time from the previous location, or to anchor the reader into the specifics of where the characters are.

Assignment

Look at the opening of each chapter of your WIP and read until you can point to specific hints that will alert the reader to the *where* and *when* of time passing since the last chapter. If these cues are not in the first few paragraphs, can you rewrite to make it easier and clearer for the reader to stay engaged?

If you feel you've done a solid job of anchoring the reader at the beginning of chapters and scenes, then give it to someone who hasn't read your work already. Using a few scene and chapter openings (no more than two or three paragraphs), ask her to highlight where she feels comfortable with the *when* and *where* of the Setting.

Look at the POV character's experience, and see how you can sneak in more details that will help the reader figure out *where* and *when*.

Recap

- The harder a reader must work to figure out the *where* and *when* of a story, the easier it is to set a book down.
- To keep your reader engaged, anchor or orient them as quickly as possible in every chapter and every change of scene.
- If you use omniscient POV, use it with a light hand.
- Study other authors to see how they approach these elements of Setting.

08

Using Setting in an Action Sequence

Be wary of writing more about the Setting than a story can handle. A short scene requires only a few words of description. If you are in the middle of an action scene, you don't necessarily want to slow the pacing to describe too much detail. There are no set rules for this, but if you work details in around the characters' actions, you should be fine.

When reading other authors' works, keep an eye out for when and where they slow the pacing to give longer descriptions, and where they increase pacing by using shorter snippets that still orient the reader. Use different colored post-it notes to mark examples and return to them after you've finished a novel to study the book in more depth.

Here's a quick example from a Lee Child thriller. At this point in the story, the POV character has arrived at a pathologist's office to ask some questions about a murder victim. It's the day after the New Year's holiday and the character already observed, "There were holiday decorations hanging from the ceiling. They looked a little tired." So the reader has seen the out-of-place decorations when this next passage occurs. The specific Setting details are contained in one sentence, with two sensory details to ramp it up and pull the reader deeper into what the POV character is experiencing.

Then she looked at each of us in turn in case we had more questions. We didn't, so she smiled once more and swept away through a door. It sucked shut behind her and the ceiling decorations rustled and stilled. Then the reception area went quiet.

—Lee Child, *The Enemy*

What if Child had written just this?

> **ROUGH DRAFT:** Then she looked at each of us in turn in case we had more questions. We didn't, so she smiled once more and swept away through a door.

See how stopping at this point doesn't pull the reader into the scene? There's no sense of finality created by using Setting details. There are no sounds, no bringing home the point that the POV character, an investigator, has hit a dead-end here. Because of only one sentence, and the details shared within it, does the reader experience this morgue, talking to a pathologist, and feeling what the character feels when the pathologist departs. So don't think an action sequence must always be long and involved. Look for the small moments to use Setting details, too.

Using Short Cues

Let's examine using short cues in an action sequence to orient and anchor the reader:

> BLASTING NORTH on the 101. Pike gave no warning before horsing across four lanes of traffic to the exit ramp. They fell off the freeway like a brick dropped in water.
>
> —Robert Crais, *The Watchman*

If the reader is familiar with Route 101 along the California coast, she probably has a stronger visual of where in the story the characters are, *but*, even if she doesn't know the area, a lot of orientation Setting details are not necessary in this particular scene. We don't need to see this particular highway in any depth to understand the story. The author is focusing the reader on the fact that the characters are evading a tail. The author could have told the reader:

FIRST DRAFT: They took evasive actions and lost the tail by exiting the freeway unexpectedly.

Sometimes that's all you need on the page. But this story is an action-packed thriller, tense with a sense of impending danger, so Crais chose to use very specific action verbs and details to paint a stronger image. Let's look more closely at how Crais did this:

Blasting [*Action verb.*] north on the 101. [*Orients the reader to the fact they are on a major highway versus a busy multilane city street. Even those readers who are not from California have a sense of this type of driving environment. Crais didn't need to write:* traveling north along the scenic winding highway called the 101. *In fact, it would have killed the pacing of this scene.*] Pike gave no warning before horsing [*Another fresh action verb.*] across four lanes of traffic [*Strong visual of what the road looks like while reinforcing that they are on a highway.*] to the exit ramp. They fell off the freeway like a brick dropped in water. [*Emotional metaphor that reinforces the action element of this setting.*]

In this next example, one from a paranormal romantic suspense novel, let's look at how the author took what could have been simply movement—characters walking from point A to point B—and instead ratcheted up the tension. With a brief paragraph, this brings the reader into the world of modern warfare and Special Ops teams. Before we jump to J.R. Ward's version, what if she wrote several drafts, until she was sure she focused the reader on the grittiness of a specific Setting, through the point of view of an experienced military operative? She might have written something like this:

FIRST DRAFT: Walking up to the village was always scary.

Telling, not showing, and the reader is only in the POV character's thoughts, not his skin or his emotions as to why approaching a village would create this response. There's definitely no image of what this village looks like.

> **SECOND DRAFT:** Like many of the desert villages, this one was small, built of mud and scrounged material, and full of potential hazards.

Better, but there's no sense of action. The reader isn't moving with the POV character, instead we are left to wait until he arrives somewhere. So let's see how Ward makes this short paragraph work harder by showing the reader what it really means to walk up to an isolated village, at night.

> The "village" was more like four crumbling stone structures and a bunch of wood-and-tarp huts. As they approached, Jim's balls went tight when his green night-vision goggles picked up movement all over the place. He hated those fucking tarps—they flapped in the wind, their shadows darting around like fast-footed people who had guns. And grenades. And all kinds of sharp and shiny.
> —J.R. Ward, *Crave*

Can you see how the author builds throughout this paragraph to leave the reader with a strong sense of a real village in the desert and what that Setting means to the character? Notice the sensory details, the emotional introspection that helps set up the mood of what it means to approach this village. Then a specific action is expanded to make clear that the fear here is legit. Let's pull the elements out piece by piece to see why this short paragraph works.

> The "village" was more like four crumbling stone structures and a bunch of wood-and-tarp huts. *[The reader now sees specific details—* crumbling stone, wood-and-tarp huts, *a detail that plays out more in the third sentence.]* As they approached, Jim's balls went tight *[Visceral emotional response here creating emotion for the reader.]*

A Writer's Guide to Active Setting

when his green night-vision goggles [*Item that clearly indicates military or clandestine maneuvers.*] picked up movement all over the place. He hated those fucking tarps [*Here readers are told how the character feels about the tarps, but there's more.*] —they flapped in the wind, their shadows darting around like fast-footed people who had guns. [*And at last it's very clear why the Setting creates conflict and tension.*] And grenades. And all kinds of sharp and shiny. [*And here it's not simply about possible men with guns, but all sorts of lethal threats.*]

The combination of specific Setting details with emotional body language and introspection creates a paragraph that makes the reader feel she is in this desert, on this operation at night, and looking around for all the threats that could appear from any direction.

Movement Through Space

When talking about movement through space, we mean a character transitioning from point A to point B, whether it's from one room to another, one area of a city to another, or one city to another. But there's more involved than simply describing point A and then giving equal description to point B. You, as the writer need to keep in mind pacing needs—is this a fact action-oriented scene, so the character needs only to focus on elements of Setting that will help him hide or disappear? Or is this a scene where the character needs to remember elements of one Setting in hindsight? Or is this movement simply to let the reader know the character is now in a new Setting? In the last case, a brief anchoring of Setting might be all that is needed.

> **NOTE:** Always keep in mind the intention of your scene when weighing what the reader needs to know about the Setting. The more details shared, the more the reader is being shown that the Setting will play out in some way deeper into the story.

Here's an example by mystery author Nevada Barr. The reader already knows the POV character is in New Orleans. The following short description not only moves the character from one location in the city to another in active movement, but weaves in details specific to this city. At the same time, Barr layers the POV character's insights about her response to the city to add a stronger sense of the emotional relationship between place and character. Nevada Barr shows the city while the protagonist, the POV character, actively moves from one location to another, following a lead:

> A horse-drawn carriage slowed cars coming from the French Market. Anna darted between two frustrated SUVs and jumped onto the sidewalk, where, if they did hit her, they'd be poaching. None of the drivers even bothered to flip her off. The Big Easy might have the highest per capita murder rate in the country, but the citizens were nice folks for all that.
>
> Sprinting through lackadaisical tourists like Drew Brees through linebackers, Anna zigged down Dumaine and into the narrow alley where the punk's dog had gone.
>
> —Nevada Barr, *Burn*

Look at everything that's being accomplished in this very active Setting description:

> A horse-drawn carriage [*Specific sight in some tourist locations.*] slowed cars coming from the French Market [*Specific place in New Orleans.*]. Anna darted [*Action verb which shows a sense of urgency.*] between two frustrated SUVs and jumped onto the sidewalk [*Jaywalking is universal to most larger cities where pedestrians often have to walk in between traffic.*], where, if they did hit her, they'd be poaching. None of the drivers even bothered to flip her off. [*Here are insights to the POV character about dealing with traffic, so we're getting some characterization and insights about her relationship with this specific city.*] The Big Easy [*Specific nickname for New Orleans.*] might have the highest per capita murder rate in

the country, but the citizens were nice folks for all that. [*Character's internalization that gives a specific impression of the people of this town, as compared to her expectations as she dodges traffic.*]

Sprinting [*Action verb revealing emotions.*] through lackadaisical tourists like Drew Brees [*Quarterback for the New Orleans Saints football team, which is again specific to this location.*] through linebackers, Anna zigged [*Action verb.*] down Dumaine [*Specific street in New Orleans.*] and into the narrow alley where the punk's dog had gone.

Let's look at how Nevada Barr might have moved from bare bones to layering Active Setting on the page in her final prose:

FIRST DRAFT: Anna followed a dog through the streets of New Orleans.

The reader knows which city she's in, but since we're deep into the story, that information has already been imparted, so it becomes redundant.

NOTE: Unless you show the reader that a character has left a Setting you established earlier in the story, repeating the fact that they are still in that Setting is like hitting them over the head and will jar him out of the story.

SECOND DRAFT: Passing the French Market as she followed a dog, Anna marveled at how different New Orleans was from her last duty station.

A little more info, but you're still leaving it completely up to the reader to experience this location in the same way as the POV character. The reader needs more specific details to be able to cue her into the world of New Orleans.

Now revisit how in the first passage Barr, by adding a few more intentional words, really brought the reader deeper into New Orleans.

NOTE: Focus on reader expectations. For some genres—historical fiction, amateur sleuth and cozy mysteries, fantasy, and science fiction—

readers tend to want a stronger experience of the world of your story. They also don't want the story to bog down in narrative details, so threading Setting through action satisfies reader expectations well.

In this next example, which is interspersed with introspection between the Setting details and the POV character, a Military Police inspector has followed the dots connecting the suspicious death of a high-ranking general and the murder of his wife all the way to a potential conspiracy in the highest echelons of the U.S. Military. The inspector has pulled strings, called in favors, and is putting his career on the line seeking answers that have brought him to a secret midnight meeting in the Pentagon.

Let's examine how the author, Lee Child, layers in Setting details that build tension and anticipation step-by-step as the character waits with baited breath.

> There were five concentric pentagon shaped corridors, called rings. My badge was good enough to get me through B, C, and D. Nothing was going to get me into the E-ring. ...
>
> I leaned against the wall. It was smooth painted concrete and it felt cold and slick. The building was silent. I could hear nothing except water in pipes and the faint rush of forced-air heating and the guard's steady breathing. The floors were shined linoleum tile and they reflected the ceiling fluorescents in a long double image that ran away to a distant vanishing point.
>
> Then at fifteen minutes past midnight I heard faraway heels echoing on the linoleum. Dress shoes, a staccato little rhythm that was part urgent and part relaxed. ... The rap of his heels on the floor was billowing out at me around an angled corner. It ran ahead of him down the deserted corridor like an early warning signal.
>
> —Lee Child, *The Enemy*

There is almost a page dedicated to this buildup using Setting. Let's pull it apart to see exactly how Active Setting is maximized. Before this page, readers watched the POV character arrive at the Pentagon; we know how much is at stake, and we tracked the character to the next point:

There were five concentric pentagon shaped corridors, called rings. My badge was good enough to get me through B, C, and D. Nothing was going to get me into the E-ring. ... [*Here the author uses Setting details to show obstacles. He cannot go to the man he wants to meet. That man must come to him, and if he doesn't want to, there's nothing the investigator can do. Brilliant use of actual details, and in using those details to build to the punch line here—*Nothing was going to get me into the E-ring.]

I leaned against the wall. [*He's shown waiting here. This is where many writers would stop, but not Child, who adds in more details. This is not a rush to the confrontation, but a slow buildup of tension.*] It was smooth painted concrete [*Now the reader can see a specific look and texture to the wall.*] and it felt cold and slick. [*And here are additional sensory details so the reader can feel himself waiting against this wall.*] The building was silent. [*The lack of auditory at this point reveals how alone the character feels.*] I could hear nothing except water in pipes and the faint rush of forced-air heating and the guard's steady breathing. [*Three different auditory details— three very specific sounds that we've all heard, but pay attention to only when there are no other distractions. These details drive home the points that he's isolated and how late it is, and lets the reader be there in the skin of the character.*] The floors were shined linoleum tile and they reflected the ceiling fluorescents in a long double image that ran away to a distant vanishing point. [*Very fresh detail that gives us a visual starting from the floor to the ceiling and this long length. This image plays out in the next chunk of Setting.*]

Then at fifteen minutes past midnight I heard faraway heels echoing on the linoleum. [*The reader has seen this hallway and now she hears it.*] Dress shoes, a staccato little rhythm that was part urgent and part relaxed. ... [*Building to anticipation of what's about to happen next. No idea if this is the man the inspector has come to see or an underling.*] The rap of his heels on the floor was billowing out at me around an angled corner. It ran ahead of him down the deserted corridor like an early warning signal. [*And two more sentences that heighten the tension while placing the reader in this hallway, not knowing what's going to happen next but bracing for the worst.]*

This is the power of Active Setting. It uses all the individual elements we focus on in this book to create narrative description that doesn't slow, or stop, the forward momentum of the story. Instead, it enhances what the reader experiences as the POV characters live through what's happening on the page.

Word Allocation in Setting Details

This next scenario also comes from a mystery novel. Mystery writers need to know how to juggle action and Setting, and there are a lot of great examples in this genre. All writers could and should use Setting with a light hand when keeping the focus on the action of a scene, but what often happens for newer writers is that the Setting is skipped altogether. That's okay for a first draft, but in a final draft you should not short-change your reader by skipping over Setting details that can enhance the reading experience.

Before we get to the final draft, let's assume the author, Julia Spencer-Fleming, needed to do some research to get her details right. In this scene, the POV character, a law enforcement officer, follows an ambulance from a small-town hospital to a location where a medical evacuation via helicopter can happen.

This might be how the author approached her initial draft.

> **FIRST DRAFT:** He drove up to Barnstrom's Field where the helicopter waited, and he watched as they loaded the injured man inside the chopper.

This is where too many writers stop and move on to using dialogue or internalization to flesh out the scene for the reader. That's a shame because, without adding too much detail, a good writer can bring this scene to life. As it is, the reader has no visual of what or where Barnstrom's Field is.

Unless it's already been described, one reader might think a playground with grass, another an old ballpark with packed dirt, while a third sees the action unfolding in a series of soccer fields. If this place did not matter to the overall story, the writer might get away with the vagueness; but if, in a few sentences or paragraphs, the writer has the characters standing on blacktop, what's going to happen with those readers who visualized something totally different? They're going to be yanked out of the story to wonder, how did the characters move from the field they envisioned to this different location?

So let's try again, with a little more detail.

> **SECOND DRAFT:** Barnstrom's Field was the length of two football fields, carved out of the southwestern portion of town behind the hospital and Gary's Full Service gas station. Fifty years ago this had been a patchwork of cornfields and grazing land for the dairy cows which most farmers there raised. In fact, this part of New York was called the Dairy Capital for a reason. About twenty years ago, the town fathers got together and decided to invest in a community area for sporting events, picnics, and a jumping off point for 5K running events and, once, a hot-air balloon rally.

If your eyes have not glazed over by this point, you're more dedicated than the average reader. In this last version there was way too much focus on the history of Barnstrom's Field. These are unimportant details that, though fascinating when the writer discovered them in her research, kill the pacing of the scene. What the author wants to convey to the reader is the action—the movement from hospital to a medical-evacuation helicopter, and then weave in a hint of the emotional tone of the Setting. Let's see how she did that.

> He followed the ambulance across the intersection and into the fire station's parking lot. Lights blazed from the station bays, burnishing the garaged fire trucks and emergency vehicles, glittering off the blaze-reflective strips on the life-flight helicopter, which was

hunkered down in the middle of the asphalt. Several firefighters stood inside their bays, watching.

—Julia Spencer-Fleming, *A Fountain Filled With Blood*

Notice how in the final version the author keeps the focus tight by using specific details that bring the Setting and the action to life. The first sentence transitions the reader from the hospital (the paragraph before) to where the characters currently are. It's telling, but that's fine, because she shows to enhance the telling. The second line is the meat of this Setting, with very specific details—lights blazing, station bays, garaged fire trucks and emergency vehicles, blaze-reflective strips, a helicopter hunkered on asphalt. This one sentence adds fresh visuals as well as a specific detail—*glittering off the blaze-reflective strips on the life-flight helicopter*—which is a shout out for any reader who has ever worked around medical evacuations. It places him, as well as the average reader, into this Setting. This is a small detail, but a telling one that not only ratchets up this Setting, but makes it feel very, very real.

> **NOTE:** Research can bring reality to a Setting, so don't neglect your research or assume that your first draft is good enough. Nothing can pull a reader out of a story faster than sloppy research.

Here's a different example from an amateur sleuth mystery. It has a slightly slower pacing because of the reader's expectations for this particular sub-genre, but the descriptive Setting still shows the reader so much. The POV character is meeting her circle of women friends the day after a young boy appeared on her doorstep, announcing he is the illegitimate child of her husband.

> **NOTE:** Different genres and their sub-genres (for example, mystery: police procedural versus cozy mystery) have different reader expectations. Be aware of them as you consider the pacing of your novel.

A Writer's Guide to Active Setting

Let's see how Nancy Pickard moves her character through a specific Setting, one that plays only a small part in the whole story. But by showing it clearly, the reader is anchored into the larger world of the POV character.

In the example that follows, Pickard lets the reader know the POV character is passing through a restaurant where she is meeting friends. After the emotional upheaval and conflict in the opening, where the character discovers her husband has an unknown illegitimate son, the description intentionally slows the pacing to indicate the POV character is going through the motions of her day, grasping for normalcy. Instead of simply describing a dining room that could be any IHOP or chain restaurant, Pickard focuses on the type of food served and where it is as the character passes it, which is a fresh and active way of placing the reader deeper in the scene.

Look at how Pickard shows the relief of the POV character in not recognizing any fellow townspeople, while at the same time showing the type of people in the area by what they are wearing and eating. Notice also how the directional internalizations keep the action moving. The character does not walk in, stop, view the restaurant, and then move forward:

> On either side of me in the restaurant, as I walked toward my pals, there were strangers in short sleeves and shorts, all of them looking like tourists; happily I didn't recognize a single face. There were chef's salads to the right of me, club sandwiches to the left, french fries all around, and many glasses of half-melted ice in sodas or weak tea. The price for our privacy was bland food.
> —Nancy Pickard, *Confession*

Now let's see how she might have originally approached this passage:

> **FIRST DRAFT:** I met my friends in the restaurant where we always met.

Stop for a minute and visualize what you think the author means here. A fast-food restaurant? A small bistro? A gathering place within a hotel where all the town's movers and shakers eat lunch? Because there's not enough detail, the reader creates a rough sketch in his own imagination. The author loses a chance to reveal character insights and characterization if she skips the Setting details. If your reader visualizes a fast-food chain restaurant, a burger joint, or a takeout sushi bar, that gives him a certain impression of your character and her world that might actually work against your story.

> **SECOND DRAFT:** I walked through the restaurant with its tables, red vinyl seats, and plastic flowers on the tabletops. It wasn't great on food but we could sit in the back room and not be disturbed.

Now you get a little more visual through some specific details. But the story feels slow because you're focused on the Setting in a vague sort of way. It lacks a strong sense of space, or at least a specific kind of space. The action also stops dead as we get the narrative description and monologue. Since this story is an amateur sleuth mystery, the reader expects to get to know the world in a deeper way, and see this particular sleuth's power of perception. The above description doesn't do that.

Once again, look back at what Pickard does so well.

NOTE: Weave Setting details into the story as the characters talk and take action versus cramming them together in a longer narrative dump.

Showing Versus Telling

Now let's move to an example where the author could have chosen to tell versus show, but by showing via action and Setting, the reader experiences the story on so many more levels. Remember, we're looking specifically at movement through the Setting. Also check the emotions created, how characterization is shown, the subtext messages, transition of time passing, and questions raised by the author that make you want to keep reading. The POV character, Pike, has been notified that an alarm was triggered in his apartment and has gone to check it out.

Let's look at how a master of Setting description approaches two short paragraphs. By slowing the reader, and showing them how Pike approaches the Setting of a potential confrontation with a person hunting him, the author reveals a lot about Pike's character. The author also builds the tension and conflict in the scene, foreshadows that the reader should take the threat seriously, and most of all, never stops the narrative flow of the story with a dump of narrative description.

> Pike watched the world grow golden, then burnish to a deep copper, then deepen with purple into a murky haze. Cars came and left. People banged through their gates, some wearing flip flops on their way to the pool. Pike watched until it was full-on dark and his world behind the green was black, and then he finally moved, rising with the slowness of melting ice. He crept along the side of his condo, checking each window as he reached it, and found that the second window had been jimmied. Raising the window had tripped Pike's alarm.
>
> Pike peered inside but saw only shadows. Nothing moved, and no sounds came from within. He removed the screen in slow motion, then slowly raised the window and lifted himself inside.
> —Robert Crais, *The Watchman*

Do you get a sense of place? Time of day? Where he lives? Sensory details? Crais gives us all this while showing the character in action as he interacts with the specific Setting. All this is accomplished with a few lines of Setting.

Let's look closely at how Crais could have led up to the passage above.

> **FIRST DRAFT:** Pike hid behind some plants and watched his own house for a long time.

Straight telling. We're not in the skin of the POV character, nor are we anchored to the passage of time or seeing Pike in action. It robs the reader of a lot of the sense of who Pike is, how he approaches a problem, and how he feels about the threat, doesn't it?

Let's try harder.

> **SECOND DRAFT:** Night replaced day as Pike waited behind some bushes, and still he watched. He waited until he was sure no one was inside and then snuck into his own place.

Crais does not risk a reader becoming confused or disoriented if they have set the book down at the end of a scene or a chapter. He makes sure that each scene and each chapter quickly anchors the reader into the POV character's skin. He reveals the passage of time since the last scene or chapter, and bam, the reader is off and running again in the story.

> **NOTE:** If you want the reader to get a sense of movement from place to place, consider using contrast to anchor the reader. For example, *Lake Wampa Wampa wasn't the largest lake in Wisconsin but it sure came close.* Now the reader has a stronger visual than a simple—*We drove past Lake Wampa Wampa.* The first example gives us enough of a visual to see the characters passing a specific type of lake. The second version only gives us a name that doesn't mean anything unless we've visited this part of Wisconsin.

Character in Action Through Setting

Here's a totally different story. Look closely at how the author, Jamie Ford, maximizes the Setting to show a character in action. Look specifically at how the character moves through this Setting, and how the author uses sensory details to increase the sense of risk and discovery, and to foreshadow that it matters where the character is going because of what he is doing to get there.

Before we get to the actual passage, let's look at how the author could have chosen to simply tell instead of showing the character experiencing a specific Setting:

FIRST DRAFT: The boy, Henry, left his house in the middle of the night.

Is there any sense of risk? Of Henry moving through space? Of subtext showing that the above action must matter to Henry? Not really. The reader is waiting to find out what happens next in a passive way. There's nothing that ties her emotionally to Henry or to what's happening in the story.

We are halfway through the story at this passage, so we don't need a lot of description as to where in the city this event is happening, but we do need to get a sense that this action by the POV character is out of character and creates a sense of risk.

SECOND DRAFT: Henry snuck out of his house via the fire escape.

Now the reader knows how the POV character moved from point A to point B, but we're not experiencing that movement along with him. Let's see how Ford makes the scene come alive by having the character move through a specific Setting:

> After briefly listening and hearing no sign of his parents, Henry opened his window and crept down the fire escape. The ladder reached only halfway to the ground but near enough to a closed dumpster for recycled tires. Henry removed his shoes and leapt for the dumpster, which made a muffled clanging as his stocking feet landed on the heavy metal lid. Getting up again would be a bit of a scramble but doable, he thought, putting his shoes back on.
> —Jamie Ford, *Hotel on the Corner of Bitter and Sweet*

Let's pull this paragraph apart to see how Ford moves the character through the Setting to advance the story.

> After briefly listening and hearing no sign of his parents, Henry opened his window and crept down the fire escape. [*This three-step description helps the reader dig deep into the scene—letting her listen for sleeping parents, feel the movement of the window, see the*

way he moves down the exit. And it's not just any exit—he didn't go through the front door but out the fire escape like a thief. Our hearts stop with Henry's for just a moment—will the parents' faces show up in the window above? This is a twelve-year-old boy who, up until this point in the story, has been very obedient and always tried to follow his father's rules to the letter, including the one that he not leave to meet the Japanese girl he's going to meet this evening. So the reader gets a stronger sense that what's about to happen matters because of what he's willing to do in leaving his home.] The ladder reached only halfway to the ground but near enough to a closed dumpster for recycled tires. Henry removed his shoes and leapt for the dumpster, *[Potential risk factor here: If the author had made this exit too easy, the reader would not have had as strong a sense that this creeping out was a big deal.]* which made a muffled clanging as his stocking feet landed on the heavy metal lid. *[Sensory detail that has you almost inhaling with the sound after all the effort to be stealthy.]* Getting up again would be a bit of a scramble but doable, he thought, putting his shoes back on. *[And this raises a story question—can and will he be able to return this way based on what's been revealed about the Setting? The fact he doesn't linger to consider this element means that what he's after is important to him.]*

At this point in the story the reader knows this young Chinese boy has never done this type of thing before. He is disobeying his parents by going see a young Japanese girl, thus raising the stakes of the story by sneaking out to do something forbidden. If the author had spent less effort describing the Setting that the young boy had to navigate, the reader would have lost a lot of the depth and layering of the emotional experience of the story.

> **NOTE:** Having your character move through Setting can be so much more than shifting them from point A to point B. Be intentional with what you want the reader to see, feel, hear, and know as a result of movement. Not every time, but when your story warrants it.

Here's another example in my fast-paced, action-adventure story, *Invisible Recruits*. Observe how I increase the tension, use internalization, and thread in a hint of humor to a situation to keep ratcheting up the risks. The female protagonist has broken into a hotel room on the orders of her superior, Stone, to hide some electronic surveillance devices. Having accomplished this, though, everything falls apart when the occupant of the room, a man named Blade, returns. She suspects he is selling top-secret information, but he is also an old friend. The reader knows the set-up by this point, which helps start the scene in tension, but notice how you get a sense of the room in an active way, without slowing the pacing:

> It was then she heard the sound. Voices raised on the other side of the main door.
>
> Blade was back.
>
> A quick scan. Not enough time to make the balcony. No room beneath the bed. Bathroom too small.
>
> Every childhood horror movie she'd ever watched flashed before her.
>
> When in doubt—
>
> She ducked behind the window draperies as the door swung open. Blade was silhouetted by the hallway light, turned away from her.
>
> He spoke guttural Russian to the two men beyond him.
>
> If he as much as glanced at the window, she was a goner. She splayed her feet sideways, hoping the material did not sway, praying he'd cross to the bathroom before doing anything else.
>
> If he found her, Stone would kill her. No, wait, Blade would kill her first, then go after Stone. Neither was a good scenario.
>
> The light blazed on, mimicking midday in August. No wimpy bulbs in this hotel.
>
> Bathroom. Bathroom. Go to the bathroom.
>
> Blade's feet crossed to where the briefcase lay on the bed. Then paused.
>
> Bathroom.

She could hear the slight click of the lock on the case opening. The sound of it being laid against the dresser.

For the love of God, go to the bathroom.

His cell phone rang.

Didn't the man have a bladder? If he were a woman, he'd have been in and out by now.

Then nothing. Total silence. Her breath backed up in her lungs. She was sure her pounding pulse could be heard, sure this whole wanting-to-do-something-vital-with-her-life theory was a big mistake.

If he as much as glanced at the window, he'd be able to see the rope dangling there, lighter than the darkness around it. When would they start making black nylon rope?

—Mary Buckham, *Invisible Recruit*

This passage needs to keep the reader in the skin of the POV character, and in her emotions and feelings, but the reader also needs to see enough of the room to experience it as she does. The reader needs to experience a sense of the secondary character moving through space and the relationship of the secondary character spatially to the POV character, to keep the story active and moving forward. The look of the hotel room is not paramount for the reader to know here. The size of the bed or the placement of the furniture is not vital, so the details can be minimized while keeping the focus on the increasing risk of being discovered in a small space. The use of the Setting is meant to heighten the conflict and make it clear that the size and limitations of the Setting are working against the POV character.

> **NOTE:** The more large chunks of narrative description used on a page, the slower the story's pacing.

Setting's Impact on Active Pacing

Setting includes much more than simple description of place. Always ask yourself if you are slowing—or worse, stopping—the story to look around. Let's see how a YA author, Suzanne Collins, kept the pace active while describing a Setting that comes into play, not only in the immediate story, but in a three-book story arc. The author shows the protagonist moving through a specific Setting and lays it out so that it matters in the larger world of the series.

But first, let's look at a hypothetical first and second draft version.

> **FIRST DRAFT:** I live in the Seam. The Meadow is outside the Seam and separated by a high fence.

How well does this example anchor you into what "living in the Seam" means? Are you moving through this space along with the POV character, or are you passively waiting for some action to happen?

> **SECOND DRAFT:** I wanted to leave the Seam, where I live and where it's pretty depressing, and go to the Meadow, even though we're not supposed to go there. I have to crawl under an electric fence that's turned off to get there.

A little better, but as a reader we're not feeling what it means to move from where this girl lives to where she's forbidden to be. So let's see how Collins moves the reader actively through space in the story and reveals so much more about the world of this POV character:

> Our house is almost at the edge of the Seam. I only have to pass a few gates to reach the scruffy field called the Meadow. Separating the Meadow from the woods, in fact enclosing all of District 12, is a high chain-link fence topped with barbed-wire loops. In theory, it's supposed to be electrified twenty-four hours a day as a deterrent to the predators that live in the woods—packs of wild dogs, lone cougars, bears—that used to threaten our streets. But since we're lucky to get two or three hours of electricity in the evenings, it's usually safe to touch. Even so, I always take a moment to listen carefully for the hum that means the fence is live. Right now, it's silent as stone. Concealed by a clump of bushes, I flatten out on my

belly and slide under a two-foot stretch that's been loose for years. There are several other weak spots in the fence, but this one is so close to home I almost always enter the woods here.

—Suzanne Collins, *The Hunger Games*

Look how much Collins accomplishes in this Setting description. She doesn't tell the reader that this dystopian world is dangerous for the young protagonist, she shows the reader by how the character moves through her world, checking out the electric fence, and being aware that going beyond that fence is dangerous.

The initial part of the narrative description is static. The reader is being told what the Seam is and how it looks. Sometimes this is necessary to a story, especially a series, but the author does not stop there. She then shifts the reader to movement through this static environment starting with the sentence, "Even so ..."

> **NOTE:** Telling and showing can make a powerful combination. Telling alone is more passive and slower paced, but sometimes, if the intention of the Setting does not impact the story, you can use telling. But if the Setting matters, then don't be afraid to show, or tell and show, for the strongest response in the reader.

What Not to Do

An example of what to avoid when using Setting in action:

> Astrid walked into the living room and noticed the couch, two chairs, and long drapes hanging at the window. All were blue in color and looked new. But there was no place to hide.

Can you see the most immediate issue? You are being focused on non-important details, given the context of the last sentence. The reader doesn't need to see the specifics in this room except for how they relate to the POV character's scene goal, which is to hide.

Let's see how the author can make the Setting matter more to the scene goal, impact the character, and reveal to the reader details that matter to the story. Let's move the character into this specific Setting to show the reader an increase in tension.

> Astrid jogged into the first room she could find with an open door. A quick scan showed her it was a living room with no clear place to hide. Why couldn't Mrs. Nix decorate in over-sized Gothic or furniture with lots of drapes and swags instead of Danish modern? What now?

The above is a lighter approach to showing the character via the Setting and would be appropriate to an amateur sleuth mystery, a chick-lit romance, or a lighter YA or Middle Grade novel. Now let's see what it would look like if you wanted to make the Setting act in opposition to the character in a stronger way for a darker mystery, suspense, or thriller story, while keeping the focus on the action.

> Astrid slipped into the dark shadows of the living room, straining to move quietly and quickly in the strange space. She slammed her knee against a chair leg and froze. Thank heavens it was padded, though it still made her limp and would leave a huge bruise. Her eyes, adjusting to the lack of light, could now see hulking outlines of an angular couch and a chair twin to the one she bashed. But she could make out nothing but Danish modern furniture, and her hopes that she might find a good hiding place dwindled.

Setting in an action sequence means never slowing the forward momentum to focus the reader on a hunk of narrative description that does not matter to the story. Narrative Setting description, by itself, only works on one level: to show your reader a room, street, etc. Active Setting means the reader never feels the story has stopped or slowed— she experiences the Setting of the story because that's what the POV characters do.

Assignment

To play with this assignment, you'll need to get deep into your POV character's skin. Ready?

Part 1

Look at a passage or setting description in your manuscript that might need a little more help to keep the reader feeling that the character is active, as opposed to stopping for sentences of description. If you find a larger chunk of Setting description, try the following: Take a chunk of setting description and have the character interact with the place or space. Let them move through it, touch an item as they pass it, and notice some detail, but only if it reveals something about them or the story.

If you need some Setting description in a passage, try weaving in a sentence or two (maximum), not back-to-back, but interwoven into what you currently have on the page.

Part 2

If you don't have anything in a WIP, consider using this passage as a writing prompt:

> The living room was larger than the average room and flowed into a hallway and two tiny bedrooms. A kitchen was to his left and a deck stretched beyond the sliding glass door.

See how you can play with these words—or your own—to put your character into the setting so the reader experiences the place and its relationship to what your character is attempting to do.

Here are some ideas to help you get started:

- Show a thief casing out the Setting.
- Show a tired mother with two small children being shown this location as a possible rental.

- Show a returning war vet with a physical disability returning to his pre-deployment pad.
- Or try all three interactions with this Setting to see how you can make the Setting reveal more.

Recap

- Great Setting involves so much more than description.
- A paragraph or more of Setting description inevitably slows pacing. Use it intentionally.
- Study the genre you want to write in to understand the genre and subgenre expectations.
- Weave Setting through action in your story so that the reader can see and experience along with the POV character.
- Make sure what you show of Setting matters to the overall story.

09

Using Setting as a Character in Your Story

When we talk about using Setting as a character in the story, we mean that these stories must happen in this particular Setting—for example, Manderley in Daphne du Maurier's novel *Rebecca*, or Jack London's *Call of the Wild*. It could also mean that the Setting becomes as familiar to the readers as the characters, if that Setting is used in a series.

Some authors use Setting as an active character in their story as opposed to a simple backdrop. Think Tony Hillerman and the Southwest, Dennis Lehane and Boston, Charlaine Harris's *True Blood* series set in the backwoods of Louisiana, Jim Butcher's *Dresden Files* in Chicago, Dana Stabenow's Kate Shugak series in southeast Alaska, and Tess Gerritson's *Rizzoli & Isles* series set in Boston. With each of these authors you can no more remove the Setting from the story than remove the protagonist. Take out either and the story flatlines and falls apart.

In other series, where the Setting is not its own character, the protagonist can move about the country or the world, depending on story needs.

NOTE: If you are writing a series where Setting acts as a character, at least the initial stories in the series should create the world. In these kinds of stories, reader expectations are to revisit the Setting, as well as the protagonist and cast of secondary characters.

When Place Matters

When Setting acts as a character in a story, you can't easily remove the stories from that place without destroying key elements of the story.

Usually in these types of stories, the reader is clued into this symbiotic relationship by having Setting introduced before the protagonists or secondary characters, or at the same time as the protagonist and in some detail so the reader is clear that the Setting matters.

The pacing is slowed early in the story in order to make it clear to the reader that the place matters—the author anchors the reader to the tone and theme of the story by going into depth when describing place.

In these stories, be aware the reader will accept slower pacing in exchange for in-depth place analysis, but only for so long. One or two long paragraphs at most, as the story opens, and then something had better happen.

Let's see how T. Jefferson Parker uses his first-hand knowledge and familiarity with the nuances of his Southern California Setting as an integral part of his novels:

> The Franciscans ruined the Indians, the Mexicans bounced the Spanish, the Anglos booted the Mexicans and named the town Newport Beach. Dredgers deepened the harbor, and the people lived off the sea. There was a commercial fleet, a good cannery, and men and women to work them. They were sturdy, independent people, uneducated but not stupid. Then the tuna disappeared, the nets rotted, and the fishermen succumbed to drink and lassitude. Two wars came and went. Tourists descended, John Wayne moved in, and property values went off the charts. Now there are more Porsches in Newport Beach than in the fatherland, and more cosmetic surgeons than in Beverly Hills. It is everything that Southern California is, in italics. There are 66,453 people here, and as in any other town, most of them are good.
>
> —T. Jefferson Parker, *Pacific Beat*

Parker uses his home turf of Southern California, specifically Orange County, as the setting for most of his stories. He draws the reader deep into the place because his characters are embedded where they live. In the example, the reader is flat-out told that this story could only happen in this Setting, and why this Setting is rich with conflict and a cast of characters who have undergone a lot of change in a short period of history. Knowing this, you expect different classes of people to rub shoulders and see sparks fly. It's implied that, while many of the people in this Setting are good, not all are, and that is the kernel of conflict. This is not a perfect place: It's rife with displacement and differing expectations, and Parker mines these differences to create taut, suspenseful novels.

Except for his Merci Rayburn series, Parker usually writes stand-alone novels with common threads of theme and place. He references why he uses Southern California for his Settings in the Frequently Asked Questions section on his website:

> Q: Why does Southern California provide such prime locations for your novels?
>
> A: Orange County is the most densely populated county in California, home to people who live in poverty as well as billionaires. It has a long history as a place for entrepreneurs, "visionaries," hustlers and the like. Government is very friendly to business. Business basically runs the government, so the government is often corrupt. ... There's a real energy in SoCal, a real buzz—people are high energy, and feel very entitled to pursue their happiness with absolute vigor. Sometimes it's comic and sometimes it's criminal. Either way, plenty of good material.

NOTE: For stories in which the Setting acts as a character, the reader needs to be shown the Setting quickly and in a way that says this story has to happen here and not anywhere else.

The next example comes from a stand-alone romance novel. In this story the Setting acts as a metaphor for a woman seeking answers about her childhood and a dramatic event that occurred then. There have always been unanswered questions for her, but now, while healing from a recent accident and trying to decide what to do next in her life, the protagonist and POV character returns to the small town in New Mexico where secrets about her past are buried.

The character is a photojournalist, so she sees the world as if through a viewfinder. In this scene she comes across the community church, which embodies so much of the history of the town. The author doesn't settle for the traditional descriptive words used to describe the unique southwest adobe building style, where the walls of the oldest buildings show the shaping by the builder's hands, and the arc of the overhead sky shows a clear and vivid blue on sunny days because of the state's altitude.

> Standing now in the high, hot sun, Tessa shaded her eyes to look at it. It was the kind of church painters could not resist, with adobe covering its curved bones like peachy flesh, exaggerated by the sharp shadow cast by that fierce sun. Over the whole stretched the plastic blue sky. Constructed simply, it had two bell towers, with a heavy pine doorway between them. A wall created a protected garden in front. A bus with its motor still running was parked in the narrow street in the rear, and milling tourists shot it from several angles.
>
> —Barbara O'Neal, *The Secret of Everything*

Look at the care and intentional Setting descriptions the author uses to paint a clear and specific image of this old church—*peachy flesh, plastic blue sky, curved bones*. The first sentences are all about what the POV character sees and how she sees it. The last three sentences contrast what has been shown with the intrusion of the modern world—bus motor running, narrow street, milling tourists. It's the sublime and the mundane smacking up against one another, all shown in one key paragraph.

Pat Conroy is an author who—while he too writes stand-alone novels—tends to use similar locations in his different work. His Southern locations are as fully fleshed and important as any of his key characters.

Conroy uses the cadence of Southern thought, speech, sense of history, and regional uniqueness not as a backdrop to his stories, but as a breeding ground for flawed characters, character expectations, conflict, and events. Conroy's same stories, if set in the Southwest or the Heartland, would not fly, because those areas have a different sense of self.

Conroy tries to impart to the reader that what is unfurling in his stories is, in large part, based on the people who grew up in this specific Setting—and how they respond to their world. He isn't aiming for a generic description of a location. He wants the reader to experience, right from the beginning, the mind-set and cadence of this unique Southern city. Let's see how he does this.

> It was my father who called the city the Mansion on the River.
>
> He was talking about Charleston, South Carolina, and he was a native son, peacock proud of a town so pretty it makes your eyes ache with pleasure just to walk down its spellbinding, narrow streets. Charleston was my father's ministry, his hobbyhorse, his quiet obsession, and the great love of his life. His bloodstream lit up my own with a passion for the city that I've never lost nor ever will. I'm Charleston-born, and bred. The city's two rivers, the Ashley and the Cooper, have flooded and shaped all the days of my life on this storied peninsula.
>
> I carry the delicate porcelain beauty of Charleston like the hinged shell of some soft-tissued mollusk. My soul is peninsula-shaped and sun-hardened and river-swollen.
>
> —Pat Conroy, *South of Broad*

Unlike the earlier Parker example in Southern California, where the characters and actions of the story evolve from the Setting, Conroy uses a slightly different approach. He uses the history of specific Southern Settings embedded into the characters themselves to create the story. Right from the beginning, it's clear the POV character knows and loves Charleston deeply. The city is as much a character in his story as the people who fill its pages. Words are lavished on the Setting itself throughout the pages to enhance that characterization.

Let's assume Conroy had to layer his writing step-by-step:

FIRST DRAFT: I grew up in Charleston, South Carolina, which is a very unique city.

As an opening, this raises no story questions, reveals little about the place and how the protagonist feels about it, or why the story must happen in this Setting. The reader does not feel that being born and raised in this Setting creates a very specific character, or that that character's choices, decisions, and actions will be a direct result of being a native-born son.

SECOND DRAFT: Charleston is a very pretty city located on a peninsula at the junction of two major rivers. People who grew up here tend to love it deeply. My father was one of those people.

The richness of language, the deep layering of emotion the character feels about his hometown, and the symbiotic relationship between place and person are still absent. We have a start, but still a rough one. Look back at exactly how Conroy uses Setting in this opening.

And here's another mystery author, whose series Setting is Chicago. But a Setting in Chicago can change from book to book, as the series reader is reminded that this city is the sum of its parts. All the different areas of Chicago must be experienced—not simply the Miracle Mile of downtown Chicago—to really understand the city. In this next passage, the protagonist visits the headquarters of a huge, family-owned conglomerate that started as one store. She is seeking funding for the basketball team of an inner-city school on the South Side of Chicago—not far from where the multibillionaire created his first store.

Like so many corporate parks, this one looked tawdry. The prairie had been stripped from the rolling hills, covered with concrete, and then a tiny bit of grass Scotch-taped in as an after thought.

By-Smart's landscaper also included a little pond as a reminder of the wetlands that used to lie out here. Beyond the wedge of brown grass, the parking lot seemed to stretch for miles, its gray surface fading into the bleak fall sky.

—Sara Paretsky, *Fire Sale*

Notice how Paretsky's character makes an observation about the changes to this area of Chicago—*prairies, rolling hills, wetlands*—and contrasts it with what she sees now—*concrete, tiny bit of grass, little pond, wedge of brown*. Many writers would skip over something as prosaic as the parking lot of a big chain retail store, but Paretsky doesn't. She uses it to illustrate the changes that have shaped the city of Chicago in a fresh and intriguing way—one that allows the reader to be deeper into the skin of the POV character and thus deeper into the world of the story.

Evocative Detailed Setting

This next passage comes from an amazing novel where the Setting is so rich, so evocative, and used on so many levels that it could be used as its own course on writing Active Setting. In this story the extended Fairchild family comes together for a wedding, but that's the bare bones of what happens over the course of several days before, during, and after the wedding. The wedding is the reason behind all the different characters being on scene, but it is through the viewpoints of numerous characters that the Setting—the world of the Mississippi Delta—is revealed. That same Setting in turn reveals personalities, emotions, conflict, and becomes a world so real, it's hard to believe you can't just step into it at any time. That's the power of Setting as a character. The reader cannot remove the characters and the events from that specific Setting without the story falling apart.

Thoughts went out of her head and the landscape filled it. In the Delta, most of the world seemed sky. The clouds were large—larger than horses or houses, larger than boats or churches or gins, larger

A Writer's Guide to Active Setting

than anything except the fields the Fairchilds planted. Her nose in the banana skin as in the cup of a lily, she watched the Delta. The land was perfectly flat and level but it shimmered like the wing of a lighted dragonfly. It seemed strummed, as though it were an instrument and something had touched it.

—Eudora Welty, *Delta Wedding*

The following example comes from a novel that earned a spot on *Time* Magazine's list of the "100 Best English-Language Novels from 1923 to 2005." There are a lot of powerful elements in this dark story—characterization, theme, author's voice—but the Setting helps enhance a savage and brutal tale.

Most of the story takes places in the American Southwest and Mexico, and this next passage reveals at a glance how the Setting is used to show the lawless, violent, and bloodthirsty world of the late nineteenth century. See if you agree:

They set forth in a crimson dawn where sky and earth closed in a razorous plane. Out there dark little archipelagos of cloud and the vast world of sand and scrub shearing upward into the shoreless void where those blue islands trembled and the earth grew uncertain, gravely canted and veering out through tinctures of rose and the dark beyond the dawn to the uttermost rebate of space.

—Cormac McCarthy, *Blood Meridian*

Let's pull this short paragraph apart to see how powerful it is:

They set forth in a crimson dawn [*Strong visual of intense color, but the author doesn't stop here.*] where sky and earth closed in a razorous plane. [*By adding this additional phrase, the awareness of sharp, deadly edges is raised. This is not a gentle description, and the author did not want a gentle feel.*] Out there dark little archipelagos of cloud [*Here the image of isolation is raised. It's not a focus on the clouds as clouds, but how isolated and alone it's possible to feel in this harsh landscape.*] and the vast world of sand and scrub shearing [*Powerful action verb.*] upward into the shoreless void [*More imagery of the*

POV character being cut adrift and alone.] where those blue islands trembled [*Powerful verb again describing clouds, whereas most writers never think to use clouds in a blue sky as a violent image.*] and the earth grew uncertain, gravely canted [*Again, specific, dark, and violent imagery.*] and veering out through tinctures of rose and the dark beyond the dawn to the uttermost rebate of space. [*And there's no doubt in a reader's mind that anything could happen in a place like this, especially dark, secret, and dangerous things.*]

What if McCarthy had held back and wrote a Setting description that focused only on the expanse of sky, clouds, and earth? He might have written something like:

FIRST DRAFT: They set forth with a crimson dawn barely peeking over the horizon, not yet brightening the isolated clouds that would come later in that huge, blue sky.

This is where many writers might start or stop, but the reader would never experience this story Setting the way the author meant it to be experienced. So what if McCarthy stepped back and decided to look at creating a stronger metaphor for his world, this time using only internalization? (Note that this next draft is intentionally long, confusing the reader and missing the power of what McCarthy captures in his approach.)

SECOND DRAFT: They set forth, riding into a razorous plane of dawn with dark little archipelagos of cloud and the vast world of earth shearing upward into the shoreless void where those blue islands trembled and the earth grew uncertain, gravely canted and veering out into the uttermost rebate of space.

This is a difficult exercise to attempt. The Setting creates the emotions at the same time the emotions of the POV character create what he sees and feels about the Setting. Try this on your own sometime when examining a book where the Setting is a character. See if you can remove the Setting details and make the narrative descriptions stay on track.

Setting in a Series

When writing a series of books based on Setting as a character, there's a chance of boring the reader by repeating the same information in a pattern. Readers are also very aware of discrepancies between books. In the first book the drugstore is shown on Main Street and is one-story high, but in book three it's now in a mall on the outskirts of town, and by book five it's gained a story in height. That won't work. Another issue that can frustrate readers is when the author forgets to incorporate Setting details at all, or rushes them, because she knows the story world so well. While the reader returning to the series understands the Setting, the reader new to the series can become lost or confused.

> **NOTE:** Confusing the reader gives him an opportunity to set your novel down. The more this happens, the easier it becomes not to pick it up again.

The following Setting example comes from the beginning of a wonderful mystery series by Margaret Maron set in North Carolina. Even before the series protagonist is brought on scene, the reader is introduced to small-town life there. The series reveals that the old way of life is rapidly changing. The author doesn't start with change, however, she starts with showing and telling the reader into how idyllic this Setting is. Later she uses contrast between the idyllic and the changes to bring home the conflict between locals with history in the area, and others to whom this is just a spot on the map. The location is fictionalized, but the feel of the Setting is very real.

Let's see how Maron shows the Setting as charming and bucolic, then shifts the Setting in increments to show that there's a serpent in Eden.

> **FIRST DRAFT:** There was a rundown mill along a small stream in Cotton Grove.

What happens for a lot of newer writers is they stop at this point. They feel they've given the name of a town and intentionally focused in on an important building that's going to be used in this story, so it's time to jump into describing the people in action. But if the reader has never been to North Carolina, or is rushed past the Setting with such vague detail that it's almost invisible, they won't understand that this specific Setting matters.

The reader is left to create his own idea of what the author means by a small stream, mill, and whatever this area of North Carolina might be like. Since the author is creating her own county for the series based on her personal experiences of living in North Carolina, she must also give readers enough Setting so that they understand that the mill and creek are important. They must realize that the larger Setting location matters to the series.

> Possum Creek trickles out of a swampy waste a little south of Raleigh. By the time it gets down to Cotton Grove, in the western part of Colleton County, it's a respectable stream, deep enough to float rafts and canoes for several miles at a stretch.
>
> The town keeps the banks mowed where the creek edges on Front Street, and it makes a pretty place to stroll in the spring, the nearest thing Cotton Creek has to a park, but the creek itself has never had much economic value. Kids and old men and an occasional woman still fish its quiet pools for sun perch or catfish, but the most work it's ever done for Cotton Grove was to turn a small gristmill built back in the 1870s a few miles south of town.
>
> When cheap electricity came to the area in the thirties, even that stopped. The mill was abandoned and its shallow dam was left for the creek to dismantle rock by rock through forty-odd spring crestings.
>
> These days, Virginia creeper and honeysuckle fight it out in the dooryard with blackberry brambles and poison ivy. Hunters and anglers may shelter beneath its rusty tin roof from unexpected thunderstorms, teenage lovers may park in the overgrown lane

on warm moonlit nights, but for years the mill has sat alone out there in the woods, tenanted only by the coons and foxes that den beneath its stone walls.

The creek does serve as boundary marker between several farms, and the opposite bank is Dancy land, though no Dancy's actually dirtied his hand there in fifty years.

Until this spring.

—Margaret Maron, *Bootlegger's Daughter*

This example is not the opening to a thriller, suspense, or fast-paced story, so if you want to write fast, this is not how you accomplish that feat. But this opening serves the genre—a cozy mystery series—and slows the reader into the pace and sensibility of a Setting that's key to the entire series.

Notice how the author orients the reader to time and location— south of Raleigh means the story is set in North Carolina. Forty years after the thirties indicates mid-1970s to early 1980s. *Until this spring* sets time of year. Adjectives used help pace the reader to the world of the South—*trickles, floats, pretty place to stroll, quiet pools, shelter, warm moonlit nights*. The description of the mill is evocative and lyrical, letting the reader know the building matters to the story, and hinting through subtext that there may be more to this building than a picturesque ruin. There's a strong sense of flow of life in this rural location, which is just what the author wants to establish in a series where the old South runs head on into the new South.

Also, note how, after the gentle, detailed description of a quiet backwater location, the author raised a great story question, foreshadowing future events by setting off a three-word sentence in its own paragraph—*Until this spring*. The reader clearly knows change of some sort is about to happen.

In the next example, now thirteen books into her series, Maron spends less page space describing what series readers already know about her Setting, instead turning a spotlight on a particular aspect of Colleton County. When she mentions "familiar" locations, she does so through internalization, or a few lines threaded through other action to make sure that new readers know where they are, but still keeps the series readers from feeling like they've been-there, seen-that.

> El Toro Negro sits next to an abandoned tobacco warehouse a few feet inside the Dobbs city limits. Back when the club catered to the country-western crowd, a mechanical bull used to be one of the attractions; but after a disgruntled customer took a sledgehammer to its motor, the bull was left behind when the club changed hands. Now it stands atop the flat roof and someone with more verve than talent has painted a picture of it on the windowless front wall. As visibly masculine as his three-dimensional counterpart overhead, the painted bull is additionally endowed with long sharp horns. He seems to snort and paw at hot desert sands although it is a frigid night and more than a thousand miles north of the border. Two weeks into January, yet a white plastic banner that reads Feliz Navidid Y Próspero Año Nuevo still hangs over the entrance. A chill wind sweeps across the gravel parking lot and sends beer cups and empty cigarette packs scudding like tumbleweeds until they catch in the bushes that line the sidewalk.
> —Margaret Maron, *Hard Row*

Notice again that Maron is using an omniscient, slower-paced opening for her series. This is consistent with earlier books in the series and slows the reader down to the pacing sensibility of her mysteries. No action-packed, big-bang opening here, but the reader quickly gains a sense that this specific place matters to the story, even if it's not a place they know from the earlier twelve books in the series.

> **NOTE:** In a series, use Setting description lightly if it's been shown in great detail in previous books. However, show enough detail that a new reader can be anchored into your larger story world.

Orienting New Readers via Setting in a Series

Let's look at another series author and how she quickly orients the reader to the world of her stories in a way that engages new readers, but doesn't bore her series readers. This example is twelve books into Dana Stabenow's mystery series. See how soon you know where the main character is and if you can get a sense of her world environment.

> Mutt leaped to the seat of the snow machine as Kate thumbed the throttle and together they roared twenty-five miles over unplowed road to Niniltna, four miles past the village to the ghost town of Kanuyaq, and up the rutted, icy path to the Step. There, Kate dismounted, postholed through the snow to the door of the Park Service's headquarters, marched down the hall to Dan O'Brian's office, walked in without knocking, sat down without invitation, and said, "Now then. Would you mind repeating to me exactly what you told Ethan Int-Hout this morning?"
> —Dana Stabenow, *A Fine and Bitter Snow*

This book is the twelfth in the series, set in Alaska, with several set in this specific village. It's okay that the new reader doesn't yet have a lot of information about Kate's isolated cabin, a strong visual of the village of Niniltna, any idea of what's meant by "the Step," or a description of the headquarters. The story starts with action—just look at the environment where a character has to travel by snowmobile for twenty-five miles to get somewhere, plus the snow is deep.

Because place is so important to this series, Stabenow spends more page space on Setting description later, feeding information to the reader through the perspective of a protagonist who loves the wilderness, the isolation, and the uniqueness that is Alaska. But she doesn't want to bore series readers with too much recap via narrative Setting description and familiar detail. If you attend a Stabenow reading you'll quickly realize that a lot of her fans read her stories not just for the mysteries but for the sense of place.

> **NOTE:** Assume your reader has never seen or been to the Setting in your story. Give them enough info to experience what you want them to, in the way you want them to experience it. The more unique it is, the more detail they might need. The earlier in the series, the more detail will be needed about reoccurring Setting.

Let's look at another example from Nevada Barr, known for writing Settings that become a strong character in her stories, even if the overall locations where the stories play out can change from story to story:

> The Rambler's headlights caught a scrap of paper nailed to a tree, a handwritten sign: REPENT. Darkness swallowed it, and Anna was left with the feeling she was surely on the road to perdition. God knew it was dark enough. Her high beams clawed the grass on the left side of the narrow lane, plowing a furrow so green it looked unnatural: neon green, acid green.
>
> At least it's in color, she thought sourly. Everything she knew— or imagined she did—about Mississippi had been gleaned from grainy black-and-white television footage of the civil rights movement in the sixties.
>
> —Nevada Barr, *Deep South*

Let's dig deeper into exactly what the author is doing by using Setting in the opening of this story, eight books into her series. This mystery author has a series of books with Park Ranger Anna Pigeon. Those who know and follow this character have to be quickly oriented into her world, and those who might have picked this up as the first Nevada Barr book they've read need a sense of who the character is, plus a strong anchoring element. So let's see how Barr accomplishes both goals for two different kinds of readers:

A Writer's Guide to Active Setting

The Rambler's headlights caught a scrap of paper nailed to a tree, a handwritten sign: REPENT. [*A very specific detail that foreshadows the theme of the story and the type of place where the story is going to happen. Also the use of a specific car model gives a hint of the personality of the driver. The individual who drives a Rambler is different than one who drives a Jeep Wrangler or a Volvo station wagon. Just a hint.*] Darkness swallowed it, and Anna was left with the feeling she was surely on the road to perdition. [*Now we have internalization from the POV character that gives the reader a stronger sense of who she is by how she feels about this particular Setting.*] God knew it was dark enough. Her high beams clawed [*Great action verb—sets a tone very different than if she used a less expressive verb like swept, lighted, or exposed.*] the grass on the left side of the narrow lane, plowing a furrow so green it looked unnatural: neon green, acid green. [*Again, more subtle internalization that lets the reader know the POV character is not necessarily comfortable with this much vegetation. Those readers who follow the series already know that Anna has spent much of her career in the West and more specifically the dry desert land of the Southwest. The reader doesn't need that much backstory here, but they do need a sense of her response to what she's seeing.*]

At least it's in color, she thought sourly. [*The reader now knows exactly how the character feels—the author showed this by Anna's internalization about the intensity and variations of the color of grass, something the average person doesn't think about if they see grass on a daily basis.*] Everything she knew—or imagined she did—about Mississippi had been gleaned from grainy black-and-white television footage of the civil rights movement in the sixties. [*And only here is the reader cued in about her emotional response to the Setting as a negative impression—the reader is shown the Setting, then told how Anna feels about it by being focused on very specific images and word choices. The reader also gets a sense of backstory of the POV character by what she watched on television as a child.*]

Here's another example from this same author. Different Setting, but still a quick and clear sense is given to the reader that the location matters to the story. It's not the river itself that matters, but the river as a metaphor for the life of this iconic city. The example also reveals that this place is not where the POV character grew up as well as showing how she feels about her new environment. See how the author weaves in the time of day and year without being specific about the place. That comes two paragraphs after this, but a careful reader can guess by noting key words long before the town's name is ever used.

> Old Man River. What a crock, Anna thought as she sat on a bench on the levee, the April sun already powerful enough to warm the faux wood slats beneath her back and thighs. The Mississippi was so unquestionably female, the great mother, a blowsy, fecund, fertile juggernaut that nurtured and destroyed with the same sublime indifference.
>
> Rivers were paltry things where Anna had grown up, fierce only when they flash-flooded. Compared to the Mississippi their occasional rampages seemed merely the peevish snits of adolescence.
> —Nevada Barr, *Burn*

Let's look at one last example to contrast to the last two. Tony Hillerman's name as an author is synonymous with the Southwest, a very different environment than the two previous examples from Barr. Hillerman weaves the Setting in on every page to make it clear to the reader that, in his series, the world of the Southwest and the land of the Navajo and Hopi are intrinsic to the stories. In this early passage from *The Wailing Wind*, a secondary character, who is a member of the Navajo Tribal police, orients readers to where the story is happening and shows them how tied she is to the land by her response to her Setting.

> She [Bernie] sat on a sandstone slab in a mixed growth of aspen and spruce … facing north to take advantage of the view. Pastora Peak and the Carrizo Mountains blocked off the Colorado Rockies. And

the Lukachuki Forest around her closed off Utah's peaks. But an infinity of New Mexico's empty corner spread below her, and to the left lay the northern half of Arizona. This immensity, dappled with cloud shadows and punctuated with assorted mountain peaks, was enough to lift the human spirit. At least it did for Bernie.

—Tony Hillerman, *The Wailing Wind*

The point to keep in mind is, if you are writing a story, or a series where the Setting is its own personality and character, you can get away with more chunks of description because the reader wants to be well anchored, not just in the story issues—the mystery, romance, suspense, etc.—but also in the world of the story.

What Not to Do

Don't assume your reader knows your Setting as well as you know it. Below are some modified examples of Setting descriptions gathered from newer writers over the years to give you an idea of the pitfalls of assuming anything.

> It was one of those West Texas sunsets.

Now, if you know West Texas well, have traveled through it, or the sunset was described earlier in your story, this might mean something. But without any of the above, the Setting description shows nothing, especially if you don't know Texas.

> He went down to Livingston Avenue.

And down means what? South? Down a hill? How far is down? Again, not enough information for the reader to experience this Setting or know that it matters.

> He stood on his porch, looking at the beautiful scenery before him, at the lake in the distance and beyond it, the mountain.

Can you as a reader tell what the POV character is seeing? What is meant by beautiful scenery? Or a lake? Is this Lake Michigan, Lake Tahoe, or Lake Ladoga? What kind of mountain is in the distance? Stone Mountain in Georgia is very different than Mount Washington in New Hampshire and nothing like Mount Rushmore, or Denali in Alaska. Did you guess correctly that this story was happening in Colorado? If you didn't, don't worry—very few readers could have guessed the location.

> **NOTE:** Give the reader enough specific detail to paint the image they need to have in order to understand your character and your story, especially if the Setting is a character itself.

Assignment

This should be an easy assignment, but it will involve a little sleuthing. Find either a stand-alone story or a series where the Setting is a character within the story. It should be a novel where the story has to play out in a particular location, because if you moved the characters into another Setting, they would lose a lot of what impacts them.

Read the story once for enjoyment, so that later you can ignore the temptation of getting lost in the story. When you revisit it, try to pull apart how the author makes the Setting its own character. Grab a highlighter to highlight the specific Setting descriptions, so the Setting information will jump out at you and read it again.

Highlight how and when the Setting is first introduced, how often the Setting plays a key role in the story, and how the author shows the reader interacting with the Setting. What types of details are revealed about the Setting and how are they shown on the page? If the story is part of a series, examine how the author introduces Setting information that you already know versus new information. Look at word, sentence, and paragraph allocation.

Then revisit your own work to see how your Setting can be enhanced.

Recap

- You'll know if a Setting is a character in your story by the need for your character to interact within that specific Setting versus any other Setting.
- If you are writing a series where readers have some knowledge of your story Setting based on earlier novels, go lightly on what you've already revealed to the reader. Then expand on an element or elements of the Setting she needs to know for this particular book in the series.
- Be specific with your details and how your characters interact with your Setting from your primary story characters. Let their interaction with the Setting, whether from a previous novel or as a new character in the series, reveal information to the reader both about themselves and the world of the story.

10

The Devil in the Setting Details

By now you should have stopped thinking of Setting as simply a way to show the reader location. Instead, think of Setting as a rich medium to use showing, not telling, to anchor the reader into the passage of time or change of place in your story, to act as its own character if the reader expects that, and, above all, to draw the reader deeper into *your* story.

Depending on the genre you're writing, the Setting details can be minimal or everything to the story. Science fiction and fantasy writers are known for their worldbuilding, creating universes populated with exotic new places and the people who inhabit them. In these genres, Setting is pivotal. Think Hogwarts in the Harry Potter stories, Middle Earth in Tolkien's Lord of the Rings series, or the world of the Hunger Games series by Suzanne Collins. Other novels can be streamlined. Harlan Coben's stand-alone thrillers tend to be minimalistic in locations—his characters are someplace in New Jersey—but the settings have more to do with creating an environment of an ordinary man as opposed to the sense that these stories *must* happen in a particular location.

The secret is to keep in mind your target audience when you're writing and be aware of the intention of your Setting. How do you figure this out? I hope you read what you write. I say that because I'm always surprised when working with writers on their manuscripts and I ask them, "What types of books are you reading?" or "What books in this genre have you read in the last year?" Often I hear, "Oh, I'm too busy to read." Or worse, they mention that the only books they have read were published ten or twenty years ago, and there was a very different pacing sensibility then. To understand what I mean, watch a TV show—even one from a series that you love—from ten or twenty years ago and see if it's easy to sit through the whole hour without wanting the story to speed up!

In the following example, the author uses a number of the techniques we've looked at closely in this book.

> A mile behind us, some local bar. Lonely way station. Out in the middle of nowhere, just a shed, neon lights shaped like a naked woman flickering on and off through the dirty-tinted glass. Nipples winking. Pickup trucks in the narrow, shoveled, salted lot. Scents of fried food and burned engine oil in my nostrils.
> —Marjorie M. Liu, *The Iron Hunt*

Let's examine this passage more closely to see how it's working so hard.

> A mile behind us [*Telling the reader, but when used with showing, a writer can tell. In this example, the reader is quickly oriented to the character's location after she has left her disabled car, without shifting the focus off the action happening.*] some local bar. Lonely way station. Out in the middle of nowhere, [*Three different descriptions that paint a very clear image of isolation, loneliness, and nondescript place—all of which add to the reader knowing of the breakdown of their car and that a mother and her daughter need help—ratchet up the conflict. This is clearly not the kind of place a mom would want to bring her daughter, but there are no other options around.*] just a shed, [*More specific visual of this bar. It's not a small-town local hangout, or a jammed truck-stop bar; it's almost like it's not even there, being only a shed.*] neon lights shaped like a naked woman flickering on and off through the dirty-tinted glass. [*Look at what the author is getting the reader to focus on—dirty windows, a naked woman sign. This is more conflict being layered in for a woman and child.*] Nipples winking. Pickup trucks in the narrow, shoveled, salt-

ed lot. [*Here the author could have stopped with pickup trucks in the lot but she didn't. She wanted the reader to see this place, to be in this place—so she added three beats*—narrow, shoveled, salted. *The last word builds on what the reader already knows, that it's wintertime and snowy. So these three words, if used differently, could shift the attention off the bar itself, bring home the point that this shed is in a very small footstep of land.*] Scents of fried food and burned engine oil in my nostrils. [*And here the sensory details build a strong image that again pulls the reader deeper into the Setting.*]

If the author had been lazy, or didn't think to use this bar as anything but a building in which to place the next action of the story, she might have written her final draft something like this:

ROUGH DRAFT: A mile behind us was a bar with neon signs and a few pickup trucks in the adjacent lot.

The tension the author creates by having two characters—a mother and her young daughter needing to find help—would be lessened because the reader could easily see a friendly neighborhood bar, where locals might go to kick back and relax. Nothing threatening there. Instead, the author draws the reader in by using a few lines of description to pull him deeper into the story—almost like a series of quick snapshots. That's all that is needed and the author transitions the reader from one Setting to another, makes that Setting specific, uses it to increase tension, and powers up the passage with sensory details. Not bad for less than a paragraph.

NOTE: In some stories the Settings are meant to be relatively unimportant, but in other stories Setting is vital to understanding everything else about the story.

Your Story, Your Setting, Is Unique

Be conscious of *your* story and its needs. Setting helps define your character—proprietor of a yarn shop in a small-town setting, law-enforcement officer in the Florida Keys, horse groomer in Billings, Montana—so make sure the reader gets a strong sense of the core Setting.

If you are writing a series, make sure you do this in your first book through all of the ways we've mentioned. Then, when you write the story Setting in future books, use a few familiar "landmarks" to orient previous readers and ground new ones, but add a fresh take—such as change of season to give the POV character a different sense of place. Or add a new Setting detail to contrast with previous stories—a new boat in the marina gives an opportunity to remind readers what the marina usually looks like, or renovations on a nearby building could be used to show how the POV character deals with changes to her everyday world. Look at how Margaret Maron did this in the examples we used earlier— showing a mill in one story, and later in the series focusing in on another building that had not yet been introduced into the series—to keep the stories fresh while at the same time familiar.

Not writing a series? You still need to keep in mind where and when you want to deepen Setting detail and when you want to keep to the bare minimum. Historical, period, or science fiction and fantasy writers must respond to their core readership who read for the time period as well as the story—many times they encourage more Setting details. I hope that after reading this book, you've found some fresh ways to get that information across instead of simply plunking down long paragraphs of visual Setting information.

> Don't tell me the moon is shining; show me the glint of light on broken glass.
> —Attributed to Anton Chekhov

Pay Attention to Setting in What You Read and Write

Read specifically for Setting. The strongest writers make Setting look so easy we can forget how important it is for story to flow. Read once for pleasure but then re-read to see how a specific author creates his world and moves the character through space without ever confusing, or losing, the reader:

> Pike moved quickly. He dropped into the condo grounds behind a flat building that faced an enormous communal swimming pool. A lush curtain of banana trees, birds-of-paradise, and canna plants hid a sound wall baffling the pool equipment, and continued around the pool and walkways.
> —Robert Crais, *The Watchman*

By using very specific, very clear descriptions of the type of foliage the POV character encounters, the author steps away from generic to real in the reader's mind. Any reader who is familiar with Southern California where this story is set is immediately pulled into the Setting by the three plant names—common enough to be familiar to a lot of readers, but specific enough to paint a strong image of this area of the world. Look at what is missing if you remove that one key line below:

> Pike moved quickly. He dropped into the condo grounds behind a flat building that faced an enormous communal swimming pool. A lush curtain of plants hid a sound wall baffling the pool equipment, and continued around the pool and walkways.

Do you "see" the Setting as well? Do you get the sense of warm humidity necessary to create a certain type of sub-tropical foliage specific to Southern California, or do your eyes glaze over at the generic description of a building, a pool, and sidewalks?

Avoid stringing a list of adjectives together. Separate the details.

NOT: The plush red chair, pushed against the wide, polished wall panels. ...

BUT: Barbara sat stone frozen on the chair and picked at the red velvet nap until a thread unraveled. She then rolled it between her fingers and pushed it flat against the cushion. Wide oak panels gave the room an oppressive feel, everything polished to a shine and reeking of Pledge.

OR:

Bracing her back against the blood-red chair, Matty hoped like hell the ancient relic didn't shed against her white sweater. Brad would decorate in dead relative cast-offs. Aunt Lulu had owned the chair, Second Cousin Fran still ate off her retro-fifties tile table, and Grandmamma Mimi's house had once boasted the oak wall panels, still polished within an inch of their arboreal past lives. Sheesh. The whole place needed to be torched. It'd do Brad a world of good to let go.

See how two very different Setting descriptions create two very different stories? The first gave sensory details and painted the emotional state of the character Barbara. The second example used the same "props" but created an impression of both Matty and Brad by how each responded to the props surrounding them.

Other Details to Remember

CONSISTENCY OF DIRECTION: Don't have a character walking away from a generically named Main Street, and then be downtown, as Main Street in most cities usually leads toward or away from a downtown. Also don't assume your reader will know what you mean by down, near, close to, far away from, etc., unless you have given the reader some stronger indications—*down the hilly road* or *near the center of town*.

PLACE NAMES: Particularly in the opening of your story, be careful not to introduce too many place names unless they matter to the story or are grouped to give a specific image.

Also, don't overload the reader's focus with extraneous names. Intentionally use a specific name, versus naming every building simply because you know the names. There's a world of difference between a character passing Don's Pharmacy—where she recalls a childhood memory from the whiff of ice-cream malts served at the soda fountain in the rear of the store—and the character passing Don's Pharmacy, the post office, the copy center, a Staples store, or a Starbucks.

USE SPECIFIC NAMES INTENTIONALLY: She passed Fred's Appliances, Wilma's Curl Up and Dye Salon, and Sam Benton's Chevy dealership. Grouped together, the function of these names is to give a certain age to the businesses based on the names, or the feel of a small town where these names might still exist.

> **NOT-SO-GOOD EXAMPLE:** She passed Blade's coffee shop, then turned the corner at the Laundromat, and walked farther down the street to St. John Vianny's church until she reached Pat's house.

In the example above, the details don't add to the story by painting a strong image or informing the reader that these locations are important to retain. Instead, you're confusing the reader by focusing them on details they don't need.

> **NOTE:** Writing place names indicates that this building or business is going to recur later and be of some importance—so the reader subconsciously tries to file the names away—unless you make it clear they are being given to paint a stronger Setting image.

Additional Setting Pitfalls

In fiction, we want to do as much as we can with as little as we can. This means not bombarding the reader with every bit of detail collected from research. That information is for the writer to use sparingly.

> **NOTE:** Too much information is an especially dangerous pitfall for historical, steampunk, and fantasy and science fiction writers.

> With regards to Setting details, make sure what a reader focuses on matters in some strong way to the story.

Write what you need in the first draft, and then while revising look for ways to show what you're telling or showing with fewer words. Expect this to be challenging at first, because it forces you to think intentionally and not simply write whatever first comes to mind.

Remember, a reader fills in most of the details automatically, seeing the story play out in his head. The writer's job is to provide just enough to get that process in motion and then get on with the narrative.

Like every other component of fiction writing, the Setting must serve the story, and never the other way around.

Wrap Up: What Makes a Great Setting

Creating and describing a great Setting can be an untapped asset in capturing the reader's imagination—and that's the primary goal of good fiction.

A great Setting for a story is unique, evocative, and memorable. If the Setting is researched, understood, and then described with skill, it will stay with the reader throughout the length of the story and beyond.

Using Setting in an active way accomplishes double and triple duty. Why waste valuable words to accomplish only one story function? Always think in terms of combining functions. Add sensory detail, characterization, and conflict with one Setting passage; and backstory, characterization, action, and orientation in another.

You should no longer think of Setting as simply describing a room, a building, or the environment in which your characters play out the events of the story. It should be so much more than that, if you work to make it so.

Lack of Setting is like going to a special event half dressed. You can do it, and some folks get away with it, but by understanding and employing Setting to its best effect in your prose, regardless of what you write, you have the opportunity to make the page come alive for your reader.

Think of Setting as you read the works of other writers—both those who employ Setting well and those who leave you hungry for more. Study both approaches to writing so you can create the kind of story that remains in a reader's mind forever.

Setting that is active never intrudes on the reader's experience of the story. It should be seen in context of the purposes of the scene. If a piece of furniture acts to conflict with the scene goal, then by all means the reader needs to see that piece of furniture. But if that furniture is described simply to let the reader know there's furniture in the room, reconsider your word allocation.

Have fun using Setting in your work and enjoy the amazing results!

Bibliography

Aguirre, Ann. *Killbox*. New York: Penguin, 2010. Print.

Andrews, Ilona. *Bayou Moon*. New York: Ace Books, 2010. Print.

Andrews, Ilona. *Fate's Edge*. New York: Ace Books, 2009. Print.

Arundhati, Roy. *The God Of Small Things*. New York: Random House, 2008. Print.

Baker, S. H. *Death of a Dancer*. Austin: Zumaya Publications, 2009. Print.

Barr, Nevada. *13 ½*. Philadelphia: Perseus Books, 2009. Print.

Barr, Nevada. *Burn*. New York: St. Martin's, 2010. Print.

Barr, Nevada. *Deep South*. New York: Berkley, 2001. Print.

Barr, Nevada. *Flashback*. New York: Berkley, 2004. Print.

Beaton, M.C. *Death of a Maid*. New York: Mysterious Press, 2007. Print.

Bourne, Joanna. *The Spymaster's Lady*. New York: Berkley 2008. Print.

Briggs, Patricia. *Moon Called*. New York: Ace, 2006. Print.

Buckham, Mary. *Invisible Journey*. Port Townsend: Cantwell Publishing, 2015. Print.

Buckham, Mary. *Invisible Recruit*. New York: Silhouette, 2006. Print

Burke, James Lee. *Pegasus Descending*. New York: Pocket, 2007. Print.

Child, Lee. *The Enemy*. New York: Bantam Dell, 2004. Print.

Coben, Harlan. *Caught*. New York: Signet, 2011. Print.

Collins, Suzanne. *The Hunger Games*. New York: Scholastic Press, 2010. Print.

Conroy, Pat. *South of Broad*. New York: Doubleday, 2008. Print.

Cottreill, Colin. *Curse of the Pogo Stick*. New York: Soho Press, 2011. Print.

Cotterill, Colin. *Love Song From A Shallow Grave*. New York: Soho Press, 2010. Print.

Crais, Robert. *The Watchman.* New York: Pocket, 2011. Print.

Crutcher, Chris. *Staying Fat for Sarah Byrnes.* New York: Harper, 2003. Print.

Dahl, Danielle A. *Sirocco.* Seattle: Coffeetown Press, 2014. Print.

Deaver, Jeffery. *The Coffin Dancer.* New York: Simon & Schuster, 1999. Print.

Evanovich, Janet. *Seven Up.* New York: St. Martin's, 2001. Print.

Ford, Jamie. *Hotel on the Corner of Bitter and Sweet.* New York: Ballantine Books, 2001. Print.

Gardiner, Meg. *China Lake.* New York: NAL, 2008. Print.

Gardiner, Meg. *The Memory Collector.* New York: Dutton Adult, 2009. Print.

Gerritsen, Tess. *Ice Cold.* New York: Ballantine, 2010. Print.

Gilman, Laura Anne. *Hard Magic.* New York: Luna, 2010. Print.

Guterson, David. *Snow Falling on Cedars.* New York: Vintage Books, 1995. Print.

Hamilton, Laurel K. *Circus of the Damned.* New York: Jove, 2002. Print.

Hamilton, Laurel K. *The Lunatic Café.* New York: Jove, 2008. Print.

Harris, Charlaine. *Dead Until Dark.* New York: Ace, 2010. Print.

Harris, Charlaine. *Shakespeare's Champion.* New York: Berkley, 2006. Print.

Harris, Charlaine. *Shakespeare's Landlord.* New York: Berkley, 2006. Print.

Hillerman, Tony. *The Wailing Wind.* New York: Harper, 2010. Print.

Kingsolver, Barbara. *Pigs in Heaven.* New York: Harper Perennial, 1994. Print.

Kingsolver, Barbara. *Prodigal Summer.* New York: Harper Perennial, 2001. Print.

Larsson, Stieg. *The Girl Who Played With Fire.* New York: Random House, 2011. Print.

LeGuin, Ursula K. *The Tombs of Atuan.* New York: Atheneum, 1971. Print.

Lehane, Dennis. *Moonlight Mile.* New York: Harper Collins, 2010. Print.

Leonard, Elmore. *Riding the Rap.* New York: William Morrow, 2012. Print.

Lethem, Jonathan. *Motherless Brooklyn.* New York: Random House, 2011. Print.

Lippman, Laura. *In A Strange City.* New York: Avon Books, 2001. Print.

Liu, Marjorie M. *Armor of Roses.* New York: Berkley, 2010. Print.

Liu, Marjorie M. *The Iron Hunt*. New York: Berkley, 2008. Print.

Ludlum, Robert. *The Icarus Agenda*. New York: Random House, 1988. Print.

Maron, Margaret. *Bootlegger's Daughter*. New York: Mysterious Press, 1992. Print.

Maron, Margaret. *Hard Row*. New York: Grand Central, 2007. Print.

Marsh, Ngaio. *Singing in the Shrouds*. New York: Harper, 2009. Print.

McCarthy, Cormac. *Blood Meridian*. New York: Vintage Press, 2010. Print.

McLinn, Patricia. *Sign Off*. Memphis: Bell Bridge Books, 2012. E-pub.

Mosley, Walter. *Cinnamon Kiss*. New York: Little, Brown and Company, 2005. Print.

O'Brien, Kevin. *Final Breath*. New York: Pinnacle, 2009. Print.

O'Neal, Barbara. *The Secret of Everything*. New York: Bantam, 2009. Print.

Paretsky, Sara. *Fire Sale*. New York: Signet, 2006. Print.

Paretsky, Sara. *Total Recall*. New York: Dell Books, 2001. Print.

Parker, T. Jefferson. *Pacific Beat*. New York: St. Martin's, 2004. Print.

Parker, T. Jefferson. *Red Light*. New York: Hyperion, 2000. Print.

Penny, Louise. *A Trick of the Light*. New York: Minotaur Books, 2011. Print.

Perry, Anne. *A Sudden Fearful Death*. New York: Ballantine Books, 1993. Print.

Pickard, Nancy. *Confession*. New York: Pocket Books, 2007. Print.

Priest, Cherie. *Dreadnought*. New York: Tor, 2010. Print.

Priest, Cherie. *Ganymeade*. New York: Tor, 2011. Print.

Raybourn, Deanna. *A Spear of Summer Grass*. Ontario: Mira, 2013. Print.

Richards, Emilie. *Fox River*. New York: Mira, 2001. Print.

Shinn, Sharon. *Wrapt in Crystal*. New York: Berkley, 1999. Print.

Simonson, Helen. *Major Pettigrew's Last Stand*. New York: Random House, 2010. Print.

Spenser-Fleming, Julia. *A Fountain Filled With Blood*. New York: Minotaur Books, 2003. Print.

Spenser-Fleming, Julia. *I Shall Not Want*. New York: Minotaur, 2008. Reprint.

Stabenow, Dana. *A Fine and Bitter Snow*. New York: Minotaur, 2003. Print.

Steinbeck, John. *Cannery Row*. New York: Bantam, 1959. Print.

Strout, Elizabeth. *Olive Kitteridge*. New York: Random House, 2008. Print.

Tan, Maureen. *AKA Jane*. New York: Warner, 1997. Print.

Tropper, Jonathan. *This is Where I Leave You*. New York: Penguin, 2009. Print.

Vargas, Fred. *The Chalk Man*. New York: Penguin, 2009. Print.

Vreeland, Susan. *The Forest Lover*. New York: Penguin, 2004. Print.

Walsh, Joyce Keller. *Strummin' The Banjo Moon*. Missouri: Solstice, 2011. Print.

Ward, J. R. *Crave*. New York: Signet, 2010. Print.

Welty, Eudora. *Delta Wedding*. New York: Harcourt Brace Jovanovich, 1979. Print.

Westerfeld, Scott. *Uglies*. New York: Simon Pulse, 2011. Print.

Wilem, Frank. *The Aral*. Deep Blue Press: Gulfport, 2014. Print.

Zusak, Markus. *The Book Thief*. New York: Random House, 2007. Print.

Index

A Writer's Guide to Active Setting

Printed in the United States
by Baker & Taylor Publisher Services